Joseph Forsyth Johnson

The natural principles lf landscape gardening:

Or, The adornment of land for perpetual beauty

Joseph Forsyth Johnson

The natural principles lf landscape gardening:
Or, The adornment of land for perpetual beauty

ISBN/EAN: 9783337728403

Printed in Europe, USA, Canada, Australia, Japan

Cover: Foto ©ninafisch / pixelio.de

More available books at **www.hansebooks.com**

THE NATURAL PRINCIPLES

OF

LANDSCAPE GARDENING:

OR

THE ADORNMENT OF LAND

FOR

PERPETUAL BEAUTY.

BY

JOSEPH FORSYTH JOHNSON,

CURATOR OF THE ROYAL BOTANIC GARDENS, BELFAST,
AND LANDSCAPE GARDENER.

PRINTED FOR THE AUTHOR, BY
ARCHER & SONS, BELFAST.
SOLD BY C. AITCHISON, 12, CASTLE PLACE, BELFAST.

PREFACE.

THE arrangement of vegetation is a matter of such moment as to require little justification in advocating its needfulness. To lovers of Nature the advantages of discussing such a subject must, in truth, be obvious; for the aim of Horticulture is to beautify the earth. Books setting forth right principles are useful to students, and, even to proficients, are not without their advantages,

When the object is once brought before the thinker's attention, he must be impressed by its importance. The intention, indeed, is no other than to enhance the productiveness of the soil, and to fitly ennoble our temporary abode. To do this effectively is to develop the thinking principle itself—to further the interests of both heart and soul. The better culture of the land, taking into account the activities and energies which it is calculated to elicit, cannot be otherwise than advantageous—cannot, in fact, fail to influence for good the life of man.

When the mind is suitably prepared, working with skill and method on the materials which have been lent for our instruction and our use, every act tends to elevate the soul. Our task, indeed, is to assist Nature, to realise some effects that perchance shall last for ages. To render natural objects yet more gracious is of greater moment than is commonly imagined, for, after all, what would life be without beauty. It is, perhaps, questionable whether any great man ever yet existed who did not love nature. In fact, in his truth to nature resides, in a sense, the secret of his greatness. Monuments of marble and bronze may excite wonder and amazement, but to develop the material world, in order to improve our thoughts, helps us to love our fellows yet better, and tends to raise the heart to God.

My inexperience in authorship has kept me from venturing to place these pages before the public at an earlier date. Of the truth of the chief of the conclusions to which I have given expression in these pages, I have for some time been convinced, and I submit them now only after a learned friend has gone carefully over the manuscript, for which I feel most deeply indebted. I beg also to express my earnest thanks to Thomas Moore, Esq., F.L.S., for looking over the proof-sheets; and to Mr. W. R. Bradshaw for his various valuable labours.

Repton seems to have been aware of the object to be gained in improving scenery when he wrote the following words:—"Landscape gardening is, if possible, to inculcate the great secret of true happiness." To gain this we must endeavour, for the general good, to develop the true beauties of the natural objects which we assume to arrange, and to display their excellencies in such a way as to make them consonant with the feelings of the human race.

AUTHOR.

July, 1874.

TABLE OF CONTENTS.

INTRODUCTION.
BOOK I.—BEAUTY.

CHAPTER 1. MATERIAL.
," 2. INTRODUCTION, LINE, AND COLOUR.
,, 3. THE FEELINGS FOR TRUE BEAUTY.
., 4. THE DETAIL OBSERVATIONS FOR BEAUTY.
,, 5. GENERAL PRINCIPLES FOR BEAUTY.

BOOK II.—LAWS OF ORDER.

CHAPTER 1. LINES OF SIGHT.
,, 2. LINES OF DISTANCE.
,, 3. PLACE.
,, 4. SITES.
,, 5. CHARACTER (TRUE).
,, 6. OUTLINES—ARRANGED FOR PERPETUAL BEAUTY.
,, 7. TIME—SUITABLY DIVIDED FOR PERPETUAL BEAUTY.

BOOK III.—PRINCIPAL EFFECTS AND STYLES OF SCENERY.

CHAPTER 1. TWELVE PRINCIPAL EFFECTS OF SCENERY, AND GENERAL LIST OF PRINCIPLES AND STYLES.
,, 2. INTRODUCTION TO STYLES AND HOME STYLE.
,, 3. SHRUBBERY STYLE.
,, 4. PARK STYLE (NATURAL).
,, 5. Do. (TOWN).
,, 6. Do. (WOODLANDS).
,, 7. Do. (PINETUM).

PLATES.

PAGE 14. PLATE No. 1. VARIOUS CHARACTERS OF OUTLINES FOR PROMONTORIES AND RECESSES.
,, 38. ,, 2. UNION OF OUTLINES.
,, 40. ,, 3. { FIG. 1. OUTLINES PRODUCING LEAST EFFECT.
,, 2. NATURE'S LAWS OF OUTLINE.
,, 3. NATURE'S GROUPING.
., 4. LAWS OF MASSING AND EXTENT.
,, 45. ,, 4. AVENUES THROUGH VEGETATION.
,, 50. ,, 5. OUTLINES OF VEGETATION UNITING TO GRASS.
,, 54. ,, 6. OUTLINES OF A REGULAR CHARACTER.
,, 58. ,, 7. OUTLINES OF WATER SUITABLE FOR VEGETATION.
,, 62. ,, 8. GROUPING VEGETATION IN CENTRE OF SCENERY.
,, 76. ,, 9. COLUMNAR PLANTS.
,, 78. ,, 10. Do., Do.
,. 67. ,, 11. VARIOUS TREES.

INDEX.

	Page.
Arrangements, General Natural,	7
— for Towns,	7
— general,	107
— should be for an object,	130
Autumn Tints,	20
Ash, Mountain,	146
Acer (Maple),	70
Abies, morinda,	75
— canadensis,	78
Agapanthus umbellatus,	138
Avenues, Natural,	102
Avenues,	145
Approach to a House,	118
Animals,	144
Beauty—how to commence seeking it,	34
— necessity for,	6
— has a substance in form and its presence denoted by colour,	16
— portions of,	28
— right feelings for,	28
— comparisons for,	31
— in general,	109
— its object,	109
— balance of,	40
— Table of principal diversifications,	111
Betula alba (Birch),	70
— pendula (Weeping Birch),	74
Biota orientalis,	77
Base of Lines of Sight,	85
Bowers,	103
Character of the land to be kept true,	8
— general,	54
— to be studied from various distances,	54
— nine features of,	55
— to be kept true, and not destroyed,	56
— of the ground undulations to be gained,	57
— should be developed,	57
— of carpeting plants,	57

INDEX.

Character of Shrubs, ... 59
— of Trees, ... 64
— two divisions of—Evergreen and Deciduous, ... 64
— true love gives a natural instinct, ... 65
— of Tabular Trees, ... 66
— of Pyramidal, ... 67
— to be true, ... 93
— must be suitable, ... 115
— untrue, ... 116
— quaint, ... 137
Colour and Line, ... 11
— denoting beauty, ... 16
— general, ... 18, 123
— strong, ... 19
— must have a principle and base, ... 19
— imparts various feelings, ... 20
— placing of, ... 20
— qualities of, ... 22
— gold, ... 23
— red, ... 24
— general, ... 55, 109
— arrangement of 109
— three divisions of 109
— principal strong light for East front, ... 129
Climate—its effects on plants, ... 43
Contrast, ... 34, 35
Conical Outlines, ... 76
Carpeting plants, ... 91
Climbers in town, of effects, ... 122
— for special effects, ... 136
Comparison of everything suitable to surroundings,... 33
— each effect must have enough to satisfaction before contrast or change is attempted, ... 33
— true and untrue, ... 60

Columnar Trees, ... 76
Cerasus lawrocerasus, ... 61
Castanea vesca (sweet chestnut), ... 70
Cedrus deodara, ... 73
Cratagus Oxyacantha stricta (plate), ... 76
— Crusgalli pyracanthifolia (plate), ... 67
Cupressus Lawsoniana (plate),... 76
— macrocarpa (plate), ... 76
Cerasus—character of, ... 137

Castlewellan Park, ... 143

Dwarf Forms of Vegetation, ... 3

Drainage, ... 10

Dutch, the—their use of the straight line, 13
— their style, ... 82

INDEX.

iii

	Page.
Drives round a Park,	13
Deciduous Shrubs, planting of,	8
Earth, the—its elementary features,	5
— as furnishing physical and mental nourishment,	6
Evelyn—his use of the straight line,	12
Effects, general,	102
— grounds of,	92
— two divisions,	88
— Winter,	91, 96
— Summer,	94
— Autumn, sub-divisions of,	96
— Spring, sub-divisions of,	98
— of fruiting plants,	137
Evergreens,	90
Expands,	105
Extents,	103
Extent—to give such without destroying the scene,	106
Experience a necessity in land decoration,	108
East front of house,	124
— strong light for,	129
Feeling, good, doing much,	17
Flower Garden,	56, 120
— formal,	107
— — their object,	119
Fagus sylvatica (Beech),	71
Fagus sylvatica pendula (Weeping Beech),	75
Fraxinus excelsior pendula (Weeping Ash),	72
Front of the House—East,	124
— West,	117
— South,	119
Food of Plants,	126
— Nature's way of supplying,	127
Gilpin—his style,	13
Guides in contrast useful for sites	48
Ground—Foundations of,	80, 123
— Arrangement of,	124
— Near a dwelling,	128
Gardening—formal,	83
— various ages of,	119
— natural,	125

INDEX

	Page.
Grouping,	102
Genista æthnensis, ...	139
Garden—reserve, ...	124
Horticulture injured by plagiarism,	2
Hogarth—his line of beauty, ...	13
Harmony,	40
Holly, ...	61
Hollyhocks,	128
Hawthorn hedge, ...	89
House—sites of,	114
— west front, ...	117
— south front,	119
— east front, ...	124
— approach to,	118
— suitable aspect for,	117
Hardy vegetation, ...	149
Ivies, ...	56
Intermediate scenery,	103
Juniperus,	77
— communis hibernica,	77
— excelsa var (plate),	76
Land, undulating,	9, 105
— in general,	108
Line, the straight,	12
— curving, ...	13
— diversifications of,	14
— forming undulations,	15
— must be governed by the water of the place, ...	15
— advantages of the bold line,	14, 15
— first thoughts suggest the use of the straight,	16
— of sight,	42, 60
— of distance, ...	44, 110
— base of line of sight,	86
— in general, ...	109
Light and Shade, ...	26, 109
Laws of Order,	42, 112
— table of principal diversifications of,...	112
— in general	4

INDEX.

	Page.
Lombardy Poplar, ...	76
Leading objects, ...	103
Materials for land decoration, ...	4
Mountain Ash,	146
Margin of Beds,	123
Nature—her beauties,	47
Outlines—decorative,	14
— of buildings,	39
— in general,	79
— important,	79
— bad,	79
— for permanent effect,	81
— principal and local effects,	84
— general and detail effects,	84
— natural, ...	83
Objects, placing of ...	49
Oaks, evergreen,	69
Principles—only intelligible to those who love nature,	1
— their importance, ...	11
Planting—man's errors therein,	3
— bold,	144
Plants—the studying of their character,	10
— give many advantages to man,	19
— their names,	54
— their food, ...	126
— as purifiers of air,	126
— must have proper space to show outlines,	83
— in middle line of sight,	122
Place,	46
Power,	35
Particular wants to be supplied,	19
Pendulous trees,	72
Pinus Pinea,	69
Populus fastigiata (plate),	71
Pinus austriaca,	78
— sylvestris (plate),	78
— laricio calabrica (plate),	78
Promontories,	102

INDEX

	Page.
Principal effects and styles of scenery,	101
Principal diversifications of scenery,	111
Parks—natural (Tollymore and Castlewellan),	143
— towns,	148
Pinetum,	153
Quercus pedunculata fastigiata (plate),	78
Roads—for convenience, &c.,	13, 146
Recesses and Promontories,	14
Recesses,	102
Recesses particular,	133
Rests,	103
Rhododendrons,	56, 62
— ground,	136
Round-headed Trees,	68
Robinia,	72
Ribes sanguinea,	137
Rosetum,	134
— climbers for,	135
Rockery,	139
Rooteries,	139
Soil, removing of,	8
— do. undulations and elevation,	9
Scenery, objects of,	5
Scenery ennobles both prince and peasant,	12
Scenery—table of principal diversification of,	111
— principal effects and styles of,	112
Scene and its outlines,	110
Spring, tree effects,	137
Sites,	48
— to be rectified,	49
— of Deciduous and Evergreen Plants,	85
Shrubs,	64, 130
Salix Russelliana (willow),	70
— (weeping,)	75
Schizostylis coccinia,	138
Scotch Fir,	139
Shadow in foregrounds,	84
Study proportion, &c.,	106
Styles,	113
— Home,	113

INDEX.

	Page.
South front of House, ...	119
Sun-light, ...	114
Surroundings should be studied, ...	131
— of middle line of sight, ..	131
Special effects in time of Trees and Shrubs,	94
— Carpeting plants,	95
Taste, ...	11
— natural and technical,	
Terraces—Italian,	16
Tabular Trees—character of,	66
Taxus, ...	61
Tilia Europea (Lime), ...	70
Thuja occidentalis (plate), ...	76
Taxus baccata fastigiata (yew),	77
— objection to, ...	132
Town Parks, ...	148
Time, ...	86, 111
— periods of, ...	87
— sub-divisions of,	94
Tree planting,	104
Terrace beds, ...	121
Tollymore Park, ...	143
Trees—South front of House ...	121
Table (or Time) of special effects of Trees and Shrubs,	94
— Carpeting plants,	95
— of principal diversifications of scenery,	111
Union, ...	36
— of parts of character,	37
— of character,	38
Ulmus campestris (elm), ...	69
— montana, ...	70
— — pendula (weeping elm),...	75
Union of Terraces to Nature, ...	120
Uniting Scenery to a Mansion, ...	115
Undulations—the principle of diversification in natural gardens,	127
Vegetable growth,	15
Vegetation, ...	116

INDEX.

	Page.
Walks—their construction and character,	10, 48, 50
— in shrubbery,	14
— private,	118
Wallflower,	16
Weeping Ash,	74
Weeping Lime,	74
Water,	104, 139
Woodlands,	150
— principal objects of,	151

THE

NATURAL PRINCIPLES

OF

LANDSCAPE GARDENING.

INTRODUCTORY.

THE following pages have been written amidst the distraction of business, and by one more accustomed to practical gardening than to handling the pen. The subject is presented in a condensed form, all superfluity of words being avoided; for, while desirous to assist others, the author does not seek to force his own views on the acceptance of his readers.

Principles are so stated as, it is hoped, to be understood. At least, it is expected that they will prove intelligible to those who have a love for Nature. As for those who have not this love, it will be difficult to impart it to them. The author does not expect to make every one understand how ground in all cases should be improved; but he is at least anxious to yield assistance to those who desire it. The perception of the beautiful cannot indeed be instilled by mere words; but to those who have this perception, some aid, perhaps, may at least be afforded in the development and direction of their efforts.

These pages have not been written merely with the design to please, but to set forth as lucidly as may be the results of the experience of many years, and to help those who are really desirous of compassing the decoration of the soil. They show how arrangements can be made in accordance with natural beauty—how to enhance without impairing the amenity of nature.

No general description of the principles on which the art of decorating ground reposes, so far as I know, has hitherto been attempted. A large amount of valuable detailed information concerning the nature and structure of plants is now yearly published; and it is really needful that gardens and estates should be arranged so as to give due effect to the character of each by plant-life.

Much mischief, undoubtedly, is often unwittingly done by bookmakers, who dish up other people's brains in such a fashion that, so far as Horticulture is concerned, one might almost as well read a romance as peruse their writings. Disgusted with plagiarism, many give up reading on these subjects altogether, and thereby lose what might prove beneficial, along with what is otherwise. It is, however, very possible to rediscover a truth that was known before.

No explanation of the art of digging or levelling has been attempted; nevertheless, this is a matter which should be well understood by every gardener. Mr. Kemp, of Birkenhead, indeed, gives excellent practical instruction concerning the different sorts of labour required in laying out gardens. Every one who contemplates anything of this kind should possess his book.

Since writing out the first outline of these pages, I have read many works on garden decoration. I cannot, however, find that much advance has been made since the days of Gilpin. In other directions, I have made myself familiar with some of Mr. Ruskin's writings, and have studied with great advantage the first volume of his "Modern Painters," a work with which I am thankful to have become acquainted. Though I differ from this writer in some points, still the true poetic spirit and feeling which breathe in his pages, possess an irresistible charm for every true lover of Nature.

So far as may be, I have avoided any undue criticism in dealing with the subject of land decoration as actually subsisting. I should not consider it quite fair to criticise places in accordance with the principles here laid down—principles many of which, so far as I know, are now set forth for the first time, although in natural scenery we continually may see them exemplified. I have written more with the object of showing how land might best be permanently improved, than with any design to effect mere changes, or to set one system above another. The different subjects connected with decorative gardening have been separately treated, which may, perhaps, in a degree, diminish the interest of the book, since in nature all effects mingle harmoniously and lovingly together.

I should, indeed, wish to see all plants enjoying sufficient space for their respective development, arrangement, and diversification, so that their several beauties and natural growth should be effectively brought out to fill up the display throughout the entire year.

The decorative gardener should never be governed by the idea that one plant is better than another, for this is quite a mistaken idea. Each plant will invariably look better in a suitable position, and to see this object properly carried out, ought to be the designer's constant care. One style of scenery alone is not sufficient, but to judge by the efforts of some, it might be supposed that one single character of scenery, and thought, and feeling were the grand necessity of life.

There are in each of us thoughts and feelings beyond all power of utterance, infinite as our very being. And there is, perhaps, no scenery in the world, this considered, that would entirely satisfy us. The beauties of nature impress the heart and mind of all, but the real life of nature is only revealed to those who love her. Many commit a most grievous error in judging Nature by cold technical laws, instead of by the law of love, and thus they never catch a glimpse of that beauty which she manifests to those, and those only, who seek her.

These pages will profit little those who are cold and indifferent to natural effects. Laws can only serve as a basis of arrangement; for after all the true arrangement must be worked out in the designer's mind.

In natural plantings, time improves what Nature has begun. In planting by the hand of man, it is too often quite otherwise. It is not by any mere process of thick and thin planting that vegetation flourishes, but only by a suitable arrangement such as will ensure the development of permanent plants year by year. This refers more particularly to the larger forms of growth.

We have many dwarf forms of vegetation adapted to cover the ground abundantly—forms that may be grown with advantage in places where it is desirable to develop and to exhibit the beauties of the larger forms of vegetation.

Grass, generally speaking, is the only dwarf form of vegetation used for this purpose with good effect. There are, however, other varieties not less suitable under certain circumstances—Heather, for example, as on the sides of mountains, and the Sedums, as covering the rocks by the sea shore.

The beauties of Nature appeal to the feelings at all ages. The child is eager to gather the daisy and the buttercup, the youth loves to roam the leafy woods, and when the world has taught its lesson to his heart he finds in the scenes of Nature a soothing balm for his weary soul. No matter how varied the tastes and feelings of mankind, all unite in their admiration of Nature; and perhaps more might be done to smooth the ills of life if a sense of the beautiful were more developed in our daily surroundings than it is.

In the decoration of land, the effects to be produced should be the subject of careful study, so that as each circling year goes by, we may realise a commensurate improvement. Progress, instead of mere change, should be our motto. In general, the land ought to be laid out so as to produce effects not calculated to last a few days only, but throughout the whole course of the year. Each succeeding season should display new forms of growth, adding their pleasing effects to the harmonies already realised, as well as to those which are to follow.

MATERIAL.—Our materials are land and water and plants (vegetation). From the arrangement of these items all our effects may be said to ensue, and therefore frequent mention will be made of one or other of them, in the course of these pages, more especially of vegetation, which, under so very many forms, makes lovely this nether world.

BEAUTY.—The object of decoration is to develop the beautiful, which it is more or less the wish of every one to realise. Beauty has much more to do with our well-being than superficial thinkers are prone to imagine. Observation and feeling, as is well known, make their impress on the spirit within us, an impress which is never obliterated. Our mental sustenance would be freer from poison than it is, were we only sedulous to avoid all evil influences, and draw from what is truly beautiful nourishment not only for our eyes but for our hearts. Beauty is an *impression* made upon the *feelings*.

LAWS.—Through observation alone, those governing laws become known to us according to which Nature arranges her materials to the wonder and admiration of all those who seek her. That the effects of vegetation should become duly conspicuous, in suitable forms and colours, is absolutely essential to natural beauty. It is also needful that there should be a fitting succession of effects, so as to render this beauty complete, and, in such wise, that it should not only become permanent but progressive year by year.

SCENERY.—Natural scenery is designed to administer satisfaction to the various feelings and emotions of our nature. Keeping this end in view, we must endeavour to realise not only superior scenery but many diversified aspects of it, each in their proper succession, mingling harmoniously together, leading our aspirings to noblest ends.

This, in brief, has been my intention. Such ideas as I may possess on the subject, I have drawn from the mighty book of Nature herself—a book which has been my study for many years, and one which lies ever open to each observant soul. I now cast this work on the stream of time, an humble, indeed a very humble, transcription of that volume wherein are thoughts that rouse, thoughts that soothe; in fine, thoughts that purify and ennoble the heart of man.

As the Bible contains a revelation of the Divine word, so this other bible is also a revealing; one addressed to the souls of men, one intended to refine and elevate, and one also that needs interpreters and expounders. A deep sense of this has indeed been chief among the weighty incentives which have induced me to draw up the following pages.

Book I.—ON BEAUTY

CHAPTER I.

MATERIALS FOR LAND DECORATION.

THE earth we inhabit has had in all ages many decorators. Had decoration, however, always been effected in accordance with natural laws, different indeed would be the aspect from that which the world now presents.

In the following pages, it will be my earnest endeavour to set forth certain principles which, I venture to hope, may in practice prove valuable in the decoration of land.

The earth's surface naturally presents to our view elementary features, which I designate land, water, and vegetable growth. In their harmonious arrangement, they are governed by the very same principles which are found to rule the universe itself. The corollaries from these principles are a frequent subject of discussion. As we cannot make the world turn round by steam, it is needful to study with the most earnest attention the ways of Nature herself, in order to gain our end, and compass beautiful results.

The earth furnishes our requisite nourishment, and some two hours, commonly speaking, are daily spent in the consumption of that nourishment. With the mind, however, it is quite otherwise; for the mind is constantly at work, and demands sustenance proportionate to its activity. The soul's action is indeed infinitely higher, and farther reaching, than any mere physical human effort. Our food once taken in and absorbed is quickly forgotten; but it seems more than probable that the food which the mind takes in is never quite forgotten. It is of vastly greater moment what kind of objects are presented to the eye, than is currently imagined; and, though every one may not concede the point, I venture to assert that Beauty is to us an absolute necessity, and its realisation, or approximate realisation, the lofty spiritual prerogative of every creature of God.

It is, then, absolutely incumbent upon us to enquire in what way it might be possible that Beauty should become the possession of all. By means of the fine arts, indeed, we gain some conception of Beauty; but it is, as it were, a distant one, visible and yet remote. But Nature's beauty is a living beauty, and penetrates with a living power into the very soul of the beholder. As Dryden tells us, "Nothing but Nature can give sincere pleasure, and where Nature is not imitated the result is grotesque."

Man's work in the production of real beauty can only be effectively compassed by strict obedience to natural laws. Nature, therefore, must, as it were, be developed by Nature, by close discernment of the various aspects and requirements of the soil, thus working in accordance with Nature's laws, and thereby learning how best to develop those beauties of which the mind of man is able to realize a conception.

In arranging for the reception of objects intended to beautify and adorn, we shall find it absolutely needful to summarise, mentally as well as with the pen, the various hills and vales, the heights and hollows, sites and views, that characterise and diversify the soil. This will prove of vast utility in meeting the difficulties of the case with a view to increase the beauty, and develop the actual capabilities of any particular spot. I shall afterwards have occasion to enlarge further on this part of my subject.

It may be all very well to some minds to overlook realities in laying out a place, and to substitute impracticable notions of their own. But we cannot, if we would, well turn mountains into valleys, or valleys into mountains. The earth's surface being composed of land and water is unavoidably unequal, and it will, therefore, be better far to endeavour to beautify the actual than to undertake to create a scene entirely opposed to Nature.

Land in the immediate vicinity of towns is, in respect of its natural forms and outlines, very frequently found deficient, and discrowned too often of almost every natural jewel, it is found absolutely needful to set about its rearrangement.

When land intended for decoration has once been selected, the first requisite will be, so to order the soil that it shall be found suitable for the reception of such objects as are meant to occupy it. Then, in respect of successive stages of gardening, the ground itself will be called upon to act a part in giving proper effect and in lending shelter and protection to the plants.

As regards the laying out of ground in town and country, the removal of soil when properly managed is not so expensive an operation as some are disposed to imagine. Many, however, who think they know what they are about, very often incur needless outlay by carting their material long distances when in reality there is no occasion for it. The object being simply to lay out the ground, judicious arrangements will often enable them to dispose of the material without taking it away to be piled up elsewhere, and removed again hereafter.

In countries where the surface is level, no attempt should be made to imitate mountain scenery. A level country has a beauty of its own, and this demands a character of treatment very different indeed from that which we should think it expedient to adopt in a district of rocks and hills. In other respects, our outlines should be gracefully bold and sweeping, and the lines of planting on the whole in accordance with the general curvature of the soil. Occasionally, also, it will be found very desirable to alter the natural lie of the land, as by forming miniature valleys, raising small hills, making breaks, and curves, concealing generally objects that do not harmonise with the scene, and thus bringing about a graceful union of the lines, suitable for effects, and for the growth of vegetation. We may also afford proper facilities for planting deciduous shrubs, many of which do not now meet the attention which their beauty deserves, partly owing to the circumstance that in winter they do not preserve the outlines of arrangement, one of the objects for which shrubs are planted. Where there is plenty of land, however, evergreens in the background sufficiently repair this drawback. On the whole, it will be found most desirable that the outline of the soil itself should be made to yield the proper assistance in our arrangement of deciduous shrubs, and all vegetation.

Sometimes high ground in the vicinity of a house, as in cases where it intercepts the view or is otherwise out of place, requires to be lowered. But this operation is rarely necessary, rising ground, especially in a level country, being extremely valuable in regard of realising graceful curves.

But it is inherent in man ever to long for that which he does not possess, and therefore it is that we occasionally witness attempts to realise level scenery even in mountainous districts, and *vice versa*. Alterations, however, are not invariably improvements; and when the feeling of novelty begins to wear off, more reasonable views concerning the matter succeed, and the mistake becomes haply apparent.

The labour and cost of removing soil is an item which cannot well be overlooked, more especially where alterations have to be effected on a large scale. Notwithstanding this, however, it is surprising how much can be done by judicious management, and by at once removing each spadeful of soil into its proper place. And thus it is that six inches of soil, as taken from the lower and added to the higher level, can be made to raise the surface one foot and even more. So again, we may further impart an apparent elevation by planting the ground with vegetations of suitable form and colour.

The forms and conditions of soil are matters very closely connected with all land decoration, and must become the subject of frequent consideration when such decoration is in question. Land, in order to be beautiful, needs to have more or less undulation. In truth, it is rarely quite level unless when it is rendered so by the busy hand of man. In studying the undulations of the soil, drainage and water effects are matters of the very greatest moment. We should also pay special attention to such elevations as it may be found desirable to plant, and such depressions as it may prove advisable to keep low. Thus, in the laying out of ornamental grounds, great advantage will often accrue by, as it were, assisting Nature, and causing the new undulations to harmonise with the existing curvature of the soil.

When properly managed, and when we have to deal with a dry subsoil, it is not so costly a matter as might be imagined to raise the ground some six feet or so. The elevation, however, should be effected in a natural manner, and generally by easy and almost imperceptible gradations. The elevation of the soil will vary according to circumstances, and likewise according to the plants meant to occupy it. When the surrounding scenery is beautiful, walks should be sometimes conducted over rising ground; but when the opposite is the case, through low ground, so as to confine the view to the scenery immediately surrounding. Walks, indeed, may occasionally, with very good results, be constructed below the general surface, and in this way material be obtained for producing desirable effects elsewhere. Walks rising and falling, in natural and easy curves, in accordance with the ground imparting a pleasing undulation to the soil, produce a very agreeable impression, and one infinitely superior to any that it is possible to obtain by massing heaps of earth in unnatural and unsightly forms amidst nearly level walks.

When the undulations of the ground have met with sufficient attention, the next matter calling for consideration is the drainage, and not only how this latter may be successfully compassed, but also, how and in what manner we may find it practicable fittingly to combine drainage and water scenery, and in this way make the best use of our materials in the development and decoration of the soil.

In studying vegetable growths, in order to realise the best and most striking effects, we shall find for the most part that these will largely depend on the period of life and growth at which plants have happened to arrive. For plants, at the various epochs of their existence, evince different characteristics, and we must learn to know them, not only in their youth, but also in their maturity and decline, in order to discern how best to realise the greatest number of agreeable effects.

In Botany, a very slight variation, indeed, in structure is sufficient to constitute a new species, variations of a more marked character constituting a difference of genus. Not a little useful information respecting arrangement may be gained from botanists, more especially in regard to those plants which are to occupy our ground line.

In studying the characters of vegetation, we shall generally find the most perfect and effective examples, not merely in specimens which are the most beautiful and attractive, but in those that are the most fully developed.

CHAPTER II.

LINE AND COLOUR.

IN order to arrange artificial scenery with advantage, we must make it a subject of incessant—I had almost said infinite—study. The realisation and successful introduction of beauty must indeed be our ceaseless aim, and, however difficult it may prove to grasp it in all its diversified bearings, it will be absolutely incumbent on us so to cultivate our powers of observation as shall best enable us to fulfil the object which we have in view, namely, the realisation of beauty. Objects of beauty indeed, as seen by the eye of man, fill the heart with noble pleasure, leading to a good end; and it must be the constant aim of all horticulturists to bring out, to realise, and to inspire, this pleasure. Therefore it is that, in the pages which follow, I have endeavoured briefly to furnish such hints as seem connected with the production of beauty.

A vast subject like this involves numerous details, principles on which all those whose ambition it is to do so, may rely for encouragement and inspiration in carrying out their work. Every one will form an opinion for himself, according to the amount of cultivated taste and skill he may happen to possess, but all will agree in acknowledging the importance of principles which are essential to the very humblest measure of success. For example, a due proportion must be observed; that balance which requires that each and every effect should hold its proper place among the rest. Beauty *per se*, as witnessed in Nature, or realised by Art, never misleads, unless when through bad habits, the weaknesses of our nature, and the want of good aspirations, needful insight and just impressions fail to be engendered. Good feelings, in truth, are just as requisite as is a clear intelligence, for the realisation of the beautiful.

Men, even the very greatest, in every age, have striven for the beautiful; all men long for it; and, as their minds may happen to be constituted in some right or wrong direction, they actually seek to compass it. The manifestation of this desire for the beautiful takes the form of what is called "taste," and, according to our pursuits and opportunities, its development is embodied in some more or less suitable fashion in our daily life. The principle of man is his soul, and it should be his constant effort, by the culture of rightful influence, to render this soul nobler and better. The mask of excellence, indeed, is sometimes assumed by the unworthy, but he who does not hold fast in his heart by that which is good, is but too apt to become in the long run the prey of some inferior and corrupting influences.

Beautiful scenery, indeed, ennobles both prince and peasant, and it is not merely those who can critically weigh and decide, but also those whose souls are open to each and every gracious influence who are impressed by it. All right thinkers have a fellowship with truth; even the false are fain to respect it. Distorted minds cannot fittingly entertain the beautiful. They may copy good ideas indeed, but must oftener fail to carry them out. True beauty appeals to our higher nature; meretricious beauty to what is low and base.

THE LINE.—The line of beauty has often been the subject of controversy. All, however, are willing to admit the superiority of curved over straight lines in respect of realising pleasing results. Straight lines, nevertheless, often prove very useful, more especially in regard to furnishing a basis for other effects in the artistic surroundings of buildings, and as servants to art generally. Occasionally it may happen, where the scenery is wild, that a small portion of level surface will very materially assist the view. Then level ground, at various elevations, will have, as it were, the effect of uniting the scenery. Lines, in one form or other, are, indeed, at the root of every arrangement. Sometimes we hear of this horticulturist or that, who is desirous of setting up one form of art at the expense of another, as the exclusive standard of perfection. Instead of this, however, we must not only have one form but many forms, each varying according to circumstances. When we turn to the early days of art—for example, Egyptian art—we not only find straight lines and level surfaces held in very high esteem, but efforts made by the workers of the time to impart a yet fuller satisfaction, and supply the deficiency in form by the addition of colour.

Evelyn used the straight line in gardening for beauty. The

Dutch have also made great use of straight lines, resorting to them in many various ways. Their example notwithstanding, straight lines are best employed as a basis, or in order to form a contrast agreeable to the eye, to see beauty thereby.

Gilpin, by selecting round-headed trees, did much towards the the introduction of a beautiful and distinctive style, well adapted for forest scenery. The old English oak *(Quercus pedunculata)* was a special favourite of his. Since his time, however, many changes have occurred in our arrangements; cold technical details too frequently usurping the place of the warm and vivid appreciation of the picturesque which is witnessed in Gilpin.

Gardens nowadays frequently manifest either a combination of lines, bearing no true relation to each other, or else such a mass of sameness that it is often with a real pleasure we make our escape from their tasteless precincts into the woods. Hogarth's line of beauty has been adopted with advantage in a variety of instances. The line, however, best suited for beautifying land is a natural line, and this, of course, should vary according to circumstances; the line of beauty, in fact, being always in accordance with the local circumstances and situation of the ground. To gain the most desirable results in a landscape we must have recourse to curved lines. In roads for conveyance it is otherwise. Here indeed the lines should not be curved so as much to increase the distance, but only enough to impart a pleasing diversity of outline, and thus make the most of the land. Lines of decoration, in regard of planting trees and otherwise, must be boldly curved, for the more numerous the outlines in proportion to the length with which we have to deal, the more beautiful will prove the results, and the greater will be the permanent satisfaction. Drives, which are frequently made to run along the side of a wood, may with much advantage be carried through it, thus creating bold and striking outlines, and preventing a wrong direction being given to the road.

A road made for the convenience of a dwelling-house ought not to be carried far out of the proper curve of convenience, unless indeed good reason can be shown for it, seeing that the principle of construction which we must hold in view is the accommodation of the household. Drives, on the other hand, round a park to show its effect may generally be made according to the scenery, so that all its beauties may be fitly seen. Walks in a shrubbery should be varied, so as to exhibit the more striking features of the ground, and display the different vegetable growths in their fullest perfection: and in respect of scenery it will be better, for the most part, that the introduction should not be too abrupt. For, as an able speaker will not, just at once, enter into the heart of his subject, but with simple yet forcible remarks will endeavour to arouse the interest of his audience ere he rivets their attention with the treasures of his eloquence, so, in like manner, should the eye and the attention, as it were, be gradually prepared, until the entire landscape shall be disclosed in all its loveliness.

Decorative outlines, when arranged in the manner above described, are susceptible of certain primary divisions. Out of the thousand varieties of curves in which outlines may be fashioned, it will be of advantage to note a few of the more distinctive forms, as yielding assistance in laying out ground, arranging proportions, and making suitable provision for the objects which we have in view.

I have drawn out the following table as an example of the outlines referred to in these pages [see PLATE I., page 14], wherein I have endeavoured to show the undoubted superiority that the bold natural lines possess over all others. Nature's outlines, however, are never in two instances quite alike, and the following suggestions are merely intended to assist as a basis in respect of arrangements for exhibiting the character of vegetable growths therein.

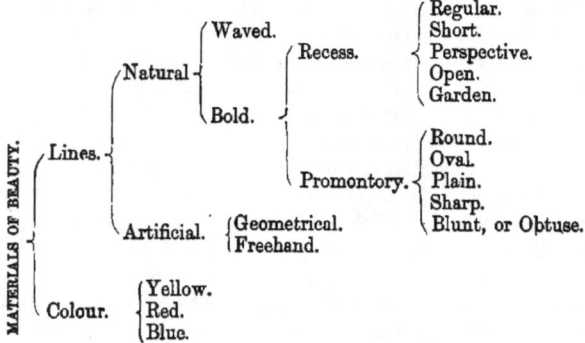

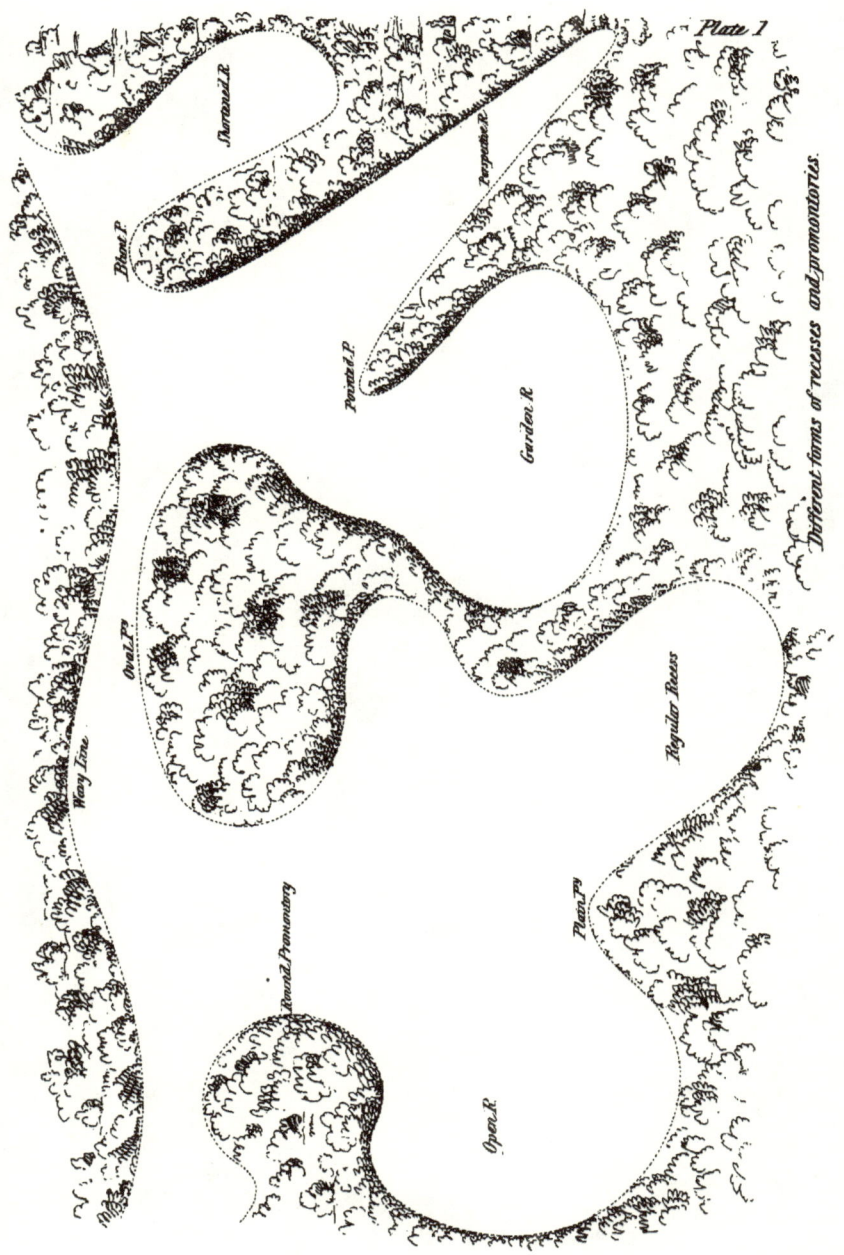

Plate 1

Different forms of recesses and promontories.

In seeking the ways of Nature in order to secure the fullest advantage from her assistance, I may state that her outlines are undulations, as Nature varies everything suitably to her purposes for us to do likewise. We must form our outlines according to the curvature required for the development of these undulations, and the outlines wanted to exhibit the forms of vegetation intended to be grown thereon. PLATE I. shows some of the varieties of outlines more or less suitable for various features of decoration. The two principal features formed may be called Recesses and Promontories, and by examining these outlines all that is necessary for the present may be understood.

Land properly arranged for beauty will have large natural forms, betraying numerous details, each plant, as it were, constituting a fresh one, and assisting in framing the general outline. We might spend whole days in the midst of well-arranged park and garden scenery, studying its various beauties, one merging into the other, and yet leave many effects unnoticed. The general outlines, as above indicated, might very easily be increased in number, but for ordinary purposes, as being of a more or less distinctive character, they will be found sufficient.

Artificial lines, geometrical and freehand, are suitable for home scenery, more especially when near buildings. Natural curves are generally considered preferable for the decoration of land, especially since the rage for abandoning straight avenues has begun. The waved line is useful in many positions when properly worked out, particularly in the details of the bold general outlines themselves. Of late years bold lines too often have been adopted when out of character and out of proportion with the surrounding scenery, diminishing in many cases the advantages which they otherwise possess. It is, indeed, most essential that true proportion—lines of distances—should be studied, and character carefully maintained, whether our arrangements be on a small or large scale.

When we study vegetable growth, it becomes at once visible what great advantages are gained by good shelter, especially in the case of many forms of plants; natural lines, as I would term them, possessing an immense superiority over others in this respect. How often are we not surprised in early spring to find nestling in nooks and corners the violet and the primrose, when but a little distance off no flowers whatever are visible. In truth, all cultivators, and every observer of Nature, will agree in acknowledging the benefits derivable from shelter. I myself have noticed the Wallflower *(Cheiranthus cheiri)* flowering all the winter through when shielded, while plants from the same nursery-bed, planted in more exposed situations, did not unfold their beauties until the month of May.

Various combinations are given in the outline figures, and explanations are furnished according to the subject. More on this head need not now be said.

Beauty might be defined as the result of a certain diversity of forms and colours, which, since it is needful that they should be studied separately, I shall treat of in different portions of this work. Forms require to be first selected to develop the character of the scene, then its details, &c., arranged by its colours, so as by their means to impart life and beauty; just as, though in a different way, the human voice and action animate the material presence of man.

In tracing the rise and progress of Art, we shall find that straight lines and level surfaces were first studied, as has been made the subject of comment by Ruskin and others. A like remark holds good in respect of Horticulture. Here also straight lines and surfaces were at one time held in much esteem, and came to be spoken of under the designation of Dutch gardening. Some, perhaps, would include Italian terraces under this title, but this would be wrong, as the latter were constructed conformably with technical art, so as to harmonise with subsisting mansions and buildings, and not to be according to Nature alone, although they have been misused for natural effect only. The gardens attached to palaces have indeed at all times been objects of much study and attention. If only as much thought had been directed to the improvement of *Natural* scenery, Horticulture, generally, would now wear a very different aspect.

Natural beauty can be made so impressive that even persons who are not actuated by good taste will often hesitate ere they alter it. Our great object indeed is to assist in the development of Nature's charms by every means in our power, and to leave them unimpaired for the benefit of generations to come. The vegetable kingdom contains a number of provinces, each of itself amply sufficient to engage attention and give exclusive occupation to many. Men of science study the structure, relations, and uses of plants; while the important work of many practical horticulturists is to assist Nature in beautifying the earth, and to call forth the loveliness that will impart life and nourishment to the soul of man. These departments, each in their several ways, are destined to yield scope and occupation for ages to come.

We are astonished to witness the progress that has been made in studying the arts of painting and architecture in various ages, and feel bound in turn to effect something other than mere change in respect of the improvement of the soil. Much, very much, may be gained by diligent study for long years to come. Great artists, indeed, have ever done so, making Nature their exemplar and directress, and her laws the basis of their works.

In observing the manner in which horticulturists have, too often, endeavoured to embellish the soil, we find that in many instances, instead of assisting, they have actually gone counter to Nature, and to all appearance have been actuated by no appreciable canon of art. On the other hand, we find cases where the arrangement is really beautiful, an instinctive feeling of love for Nature having unwittingly guided the operator's hand. In fact, when good feeling and correct observation are the rule, results will follow frequently much surpassing our expectations.

Horticulture, in its wide domain, is but too often much beyond the grasp of some who have made its study the business of their lives. Indeed, it is my firm conviction, that no art requires greater insight in those whose profession it is than that of Horticulture. It is not, however, my intention to waste time in cavil and personalities, but, instead, endeavour to explain, as best I may, how, as it appears to me, outlines and surfaces may be made the most of. The arrangement of lines and level surfaces in gardens, running as it were in every direction, too frequently impresses one very painfully. There is no harmony of proportion, or suitable arrangement of the different subjects, either singly or in succession. Persons who decorate after this fashion may, indeed, possess a labourer's skill, and twist things about, but, as for true perception of natural requirements, they display but little. Some again there are who indeed vary their lines, but without the production of true or desirable results. Their arrangements fail to impress us, and we leave the scene which they have laid out with only the recollection of their shortcomings. Decorators of this stamp may indeed possess a technical knowledge, but this singly is not sufficient. The spirit of Nature does not light up their work, but leaves it cold and dead. Some in truth have a slight knowledge of effects, a knowledge bounded by some particular principle, and gratefully receive any suggestion which relates to it, but ignore utterly the fact that beauty has many sides, each as deserving of consideration as the other.

Men very often endowed with a considerable clearness of perception, but of limited attainments, will nevertheless carry out arrangements the most faulty. Some indeed, of rude perceptions, whatever cloak they may wear, lapse into utter coarseness. Their contrasts are outrageously violent, and their arrangements utterly unfitted for the realisation of beauty and its diverse requirements.

These drawbacks notwithstanding, decorators such as I have described are worthy of our sympathy, for each one, though in a limited way, has an ideal of some particular principle of perfection of his own, which in many cases enables him to produce pleasing, if not always noble, results.

Some of the greatest mistakes are committed by persons who are wholly unaware of the laws of horticultural decoration. Being, however, the possessors of money, they are able to carry their misconceptions into practice. These persons are sometimes prone to ignore the abilities of others, and thus lapse into errors which might have been readily avoided. There are numerous localities around and about our large towns which bear witness to the truth of these statements. I might indeed fill pages in noting and describing the various tastes of decorators, but enough of the subject in this place.

Beauty results from diversity of form, the harmonious blending of a multitude of particulars, some of which will be explained in due course.

COLOUR.—Some people ride their hobby very hard; such, for example, as ignore all colours but gray, and, whatever may be urged, resist every conviction except their own. The forms and colours of earth are numerous indeed, and all the beauty which we witness is their necessary result. In other respects, our perception of this beauty must depend upon the tone of mind which we possess.

Foliage plants have been treated with undeserved contempt in the pages of writers who study Horticulture in books more than in Nature. Upwards of twenty years ago, I can remember gardeners, esteemed to be good practical men, turning with disdain from the most lovely foliage plants, while they would often spend hours in discussing the question of the colours of the flowers, and their effects when massed together. Colour, both in leaf and in flower, is without doubt very important in all cases wherein we have to study the decoration of the ground. Botanists show us that flowers are but leaves in another form, designed for wise purposes of reproduction. Nature, in truth, has sometimes seen fit only to impart brilliant colour to the leaves; the flowers in this case, as regards any effect, generally remaining insignificant.

Plants, as is well known, are constituted to draw their nourishment from earth, water, and air. Plant life is most essential to us, as supplying nourishment to animals, which in their turn furnish food for man. Vegetable growths generally purify the air, and the larger forms tend to equalise temperature and climate. Vegetable structures, furthermore, subserve an infinity of useful purposes. They even minister to our moral well-being. Great men in every age have drawn comfort and inspiration from Nature's pages.

Often when turning over the pages of some horticultural periodical, we find the claims of one plant quite ignored, for the purpose of setting up of another to receive undue attention. Instead of this, how much better would it be were the several good qualities of the plants themselves set forth, and the reader allowed to form an opinion for himself. For example, how often when one is desirous of forming a Rose garden, and, in quest of information, applies to what is deemed a good source, will he be furnished with a list of Roses, quite suitable, indeed, for the exhibition table, but not at all adapted for the groups of a garden. Vegetable structures must indeed be appreciated and cherished in all their infinitely varied details, if only we would turn their marvellous beauty to the best and fullest account.

Would we suitably impart a glow of colour to our scenery, we must study well its character. It will not be advisable to resort to one hue only, but to make one colour the principle of each sub-general effect, and others subservient thereto. We may produce an excellent effect by making use of Rhododendrons as a base or ground for the display of strong colours, or dark-foliaged plants aided by golden-hued, the latter being mostly employed in indicating the more prominent outlines. Where the scene is extensive, we may have recourse to more than one well-defined tint, in addition to others kept in subordinate. Still, it is necessary to rely upon one leading colour in order to assure the desired result.

Golden shades impart rich effects, but each and every hue exerts an influence proper to itself. Silver, for example, brings out a sense of lightness and grace; dark shades import meditation; scarlet gives brilliancy, and gray rest; brown indicates a subdued richness; purple, a refined awe. In short, the several vegetable hues originate results of varying character, according to their arrangement. Colour in a landscape may well be compared to the eye in the animal framework, or the diamond which glitters in a lady's dress, imparting light and brilliancy to the whole.

Ideas, to a large extent, are filtered into people's minds through the medium of outward objects, and it is of very great importance indeed, as regards our moral and spiritual well-being, that these objects should inspire that which is beautiful and true.

Though it may not be our privilege to paint like Turner, or use the pen with Ruskin's magic power, yet it may not the less prove our high prerogative, through the medium of our works, to impart many an elevated and heart-inspiring thought. It is too true, indeed, that now and then faulty impressions alone are gathered from books and paintings; but we are not the less bound, in one case as in the other, to contribute, as far as may be in our power, to the great sum of human progress.

But to return to our subject, it is with me a frequent matter for conjecture how it is that, seeing the intimate connection that subsists between form and colour, even strong colours, the claims of the latter are so very frequently set aside by writers on Horticulture, who call for dull tints and sombre shades as though these were the only sum of artistic perfection.

We may not hope to realise in full the autumnal tints of the great forests of Norway, or the glorious hues of the Maple and other trees in the American forests; but still, we may have a very great share of autumnal tints in the russet, purple, scarlet, and golden hues of our own various forest trees as the cool days return. The Virginian-creeper, the Birch, the Liquidambar, display clusters like glittering coins, or the golden sunset itself. The Lime yields tints, mottled with auburn, amber, and burnished copper. The genus Pyrus and others are worthy of attention, in respect to the realisation of a glowing autumnal leafage; and the colours of both fruit and leaf are sometimes perfectly glorious.

Masses of scarlet and yellow yield splendid materials to work with, and, when arranged as boundaries to a centre of delicate and cooling tints, produce excellent effects. When, however, instead of this, we group yellow and scarlet in the centre of a garden, and place duller shades on the boundary line, the result will, for the most part, prove a sort of glare. When we design a brilliant centre in a flower garden, it should be our care to furnish a still more brilliant boundary. Another thing to be borne well in mind is that, as a general rule, not more than two primary colours should be resorted to, at one time, in the decoration of our beds. Shades of these, however, may be made to blend with effect.

It is useless and undesirable to attempt to group all colours in one bed or border, and in general it should be our aim not to decorate one part of a garden at the expense of another, but to arrange so that there should be a pleasing and harmonious distribution of effects throughout.

If those writers on Horticulture who so declaim against the use of colour, would but take the trouble to visit the picture galleries in London or elsewhere, and see the marvellous effects wrought out by Titian and other great masters,—or, better still, if they would rise and see the glories of sunrise on a summer morn,—it would, I believe, do much to awaken in them a sense of the importance of an element which, in its manifold effects, has proved the source of the utmost happiness to countless thousands in ages past, and, as our knowledge increases, will doubtless continue to do so to a yet greater extent in ages to come.

We often see most excellent results produced on but a few yards of canvas, vividly recalling, if indeed falling short of Nature's infinite loveliness. But even the best artists can but give one truthful expression at a time, whereas a good natural landscape arranger has it in his power to elicit several striking results in one and the same scene, and always suitable in character to the elements for the time being. In other respects, all our doings must be rigidly true to Nature, for where falsity enters, beauty vanishes.

When two or more colours are in combination, each takes something from the other, and loses in part its original character: thus blue and yellow, when blended, form green. According to the proportions in which colours are mixed, will be the result produced. In arranging for general effect—for example, an extended Home scene—it is well to provide some simple introduction. Repose should mark the foreground, and manifold variety the distant boundaries. For remoter outlines, the primaries are best; secondary shades best suit the intermediate spaces.

Each division should be brought well out, and yet not be permitted to mar collateral arrangements. A proper study of the laws of colour, in grouping, will always prevent this. No progress, indeed, can well be made in any art without the knowledge and practice of principles which it has taken ages to discover and establish. We may never create a new world; but, with boundless materials at hand, it is within our power to beautify and adorn the earth we live in, to an almost unlimited extent. Colour is of great importance in developing outline and form. In respect of subordinate tints, dark shades impart a sense of depression, and lighter ones of elevation. It is now generally well known that all colours can be traced back to one of the three primaries—that is, to red, blue, yellow, as set forth by Chevreuil. Blue seems to retire, as it were, from the eye, and exerts a sort of cooling influence, which renders it better adapted for being used in large masses than either red or yellow. Red has the most brilliant effect, and has a greater fixity of position than its fellows. Yellow might, perhaps, be termed an advancing colour, drawing objects nearer to the eye. It is owing to this property that artists recommend a golden ground for designs. We have a greater command, however, over yellow than gold in the various forms of plant life.

The attention may sometimes be directed to beautiful but subdued tints in trees and shrubs by means of some striking and attractive colour, the latter serving as a sort of introduction to the scene. The amount of colour, however, for this purpose need not be great. I have seen a single fine plant of the *Aucuba japonica* so placed that the passer-by almost invariably stopped to admire, not so much the *Aucuba* itself, as the beautiful and various foliage, then first, as it were, rendered visible to him. After a little, indeed, the fact becomes obvious that it was the attraction exercised by the *Aucuba* that served to conduct the eye to the other and less immediately striking tints. Scenery, indeed, as a general rule, should be so arranged as to attract the attention of the spectator, either in the manner I have mentioned, or in some other. Unless this be done, its beauty, however great, will be of little avail.

Colouring does not receive that degree of attention which the subject so well deserves, as may often be seen exemplified in our parks. People used generally to follow Gilpin's style alone; but to attempt to realise his effects alone, I venture to say, is a mistake, as we have a great many plants well worth development, giving effects quite different from those which he had. In general, our season of tree colouring averages a good fortnight or so in about six years. Warm, bright, calm autumns, indeed, are indispensably requisite for good autumnal effects. In our home vegetation, we have trees sufficiently distinct in hue not only to diversify our foliage with a sufficient alternation of tints in summer, but also to warm up our winter scenery as well. One is at times quite disgusted with the wrong uses of colour. All strong effects, indeed, in proportion to their amount, intensify the mischiefs which they engender. Hence it is, as has already been observed, that many would reject the use of colour altogether, simply because they are unable to realise its proper adjustment.

Gold is one of the very best of all the foliage colours which our hardy vegetation possesses, and for the darker hues is, indeed, quite indispensable. It is important, however, to bear in mind that a lesser amount of this, than any other colour possessing a developing power of its own, is enough. A little, indeed, suffices to impart effect. When the material is of a golden yellow, as shown by comparison with sterling coin, then a much larger quantity, unless some circumstance forbid, may often be used with satisfactory results. Those who are acquainted with the arrangement of flower gardens well know the ill effects sometimes occasioned by the yellow Calceolaria, for example, in the centre of beds, and yet if replaced by "Gold Chain Geraniums" the effect will often be excellent.

When we desire to offer something suggestive, or to arrange for great displays, golden tints are the very best to employ; taking care, at the same time, to darken the recesses with retiring hues. Nature offers a very great variety of golden effects—some permanent, others fleeting; and it never proves needful, even over large spaces, to have recourse to the same material a second time. No matter how pleasing in the first instance, it becomes wearisome to the eye if continually repeated. It is, indeed, ever preferable that each scene should preserve as much as possible a distinctive character.

Amongst our deciduous trees, the *Populus balsamifera* is excellent in respect of early yellow tints. For winter, the *Salix montana*, the *Salix vitellina*, and others, and *Fraxinus aucubæfolia* realise good results when suitably adjusted. Among evergreens Hollies (especially the variety known as the Golden Queen) are extremely valuable in all their varying lights and shades. Several varieties of *Taxus* yield rich effects of gold. They are often grown in beautiful column-like forms, which adapt them particularly well for sharp corners, projections in shrubberies, and the like. Some of our later importations from Japan—for example, the *Retinosporas*—assume lovely golden tints, while in May the Laburnum realises an unspeakable and never-to-be-forgotten charm when arranging in natural massing lines. There is also reason to expect, judging by the reports from the various Pinetums in the country, that some, at least, among our Coniferæ may present us with bright and varied colours: such as the silvery tint met with in *Abies Douglasii Stairii*, raised at Castle Kennedy by Mr. Fowler.

Considering how vastly dependent form is on colour, we should study, both in our transitory and permanent arrangements, to impart the very best effects in our power. Each and every growth has a tint of its own, whether striking or subdued, and care should be taken to place it where it may be fitly developed, and in character with its surroundings, before the eyes of mankind. Tints and shades vary in the vegetable world almost to infinity; and if only we would learn to know them thoroughly, we must study them assiduously at all times and seasons. Each plant, indeed, exhibits many and different aspects during the period of its existence.

Deep tints of red are displayed in winter by many deciduous trees—for example, in varieties of the *Salix*; and the shrub termed the

Red Dogwood *(Cornus alba)* also presents us with the well-known brilliant effects of its bright red bark. When the spring begins, the flowers, with all their various hues, show forth their beauty, which continues more or less throughout the summer. The scarlet Thorns, Horse Chestnuts, Pelargoniums, along with a perfect host of what we term carpeting plants, vie with each other in lighting up our gardens and pleasure grounds. In autumn the tints are almost bewildering, every tree, nay, every leaf, presenting a fresh variety. Shades of red are shown in the American Oak *(Quercus coccinea)*, the English Elm *(Ulmus campestris)*, and the common Beech *(Fagus sylvatica)*. Many shrubs, both evergreen and deciduous, display in autumn and winter their scarlet fruitage, producing effects which are justly admired.

A lengthened list of plant names can easily enough be made out by any student of scenery. This, however, should not only specify the different colours, but the period of their appearance, with a view to the decoration of large spaces. An inexperienced person might readily enough imagine that effects which had proved suitable in one situation should change their chaarcter in another. This conclusion, however, further observation would modify. The lines of sight, indeed, always vary with the distance, as effects themselves are found to vary; but careful study of the laws of grouping, will enable us to make our arrangements beautiful from every necessary point of view.

The office of colour is to attract the attention to forms which, each in its turn, are calculated to yield satisfaction. Hues mutually blending, influence and subdue one another. The relative as well as the absolute value of each tint should receive distinct consideration. In all our arrangements we must endeavour to avoid confusion, bearing, however, in mind, as already observed, that yellow seems to approach the eye, red to retain its position, blue to retire, while dark shades impart depth, and light tints elevation. Every tract of land is more or less a foreground to other scenery, and a dark foreground will in general, make distant elevations look higher and fairer. The best rules for colour are likewise the simplest. It is well, however, to hold our strong effects, as it were, in reserve, using them only occasionally, lighting up our dark foregrounds with golden hues, the intermediate spaces with scarlet, the more distant ones with blue, and making this treatment of the several colours, each in its own position, our ruling principle.

There are many different ways of developing distant scenery, and we must, in the main, be guided by circumstances which no instructions can entirely enable us to foresee. The first requirement, though no exact rules can be laid down, is, that the form should be correct. The outlines may thus occasionally curve from a hollow to a rising ground, and conversely. Judicious planting always harmonises scenery; colour also, in a foreground, will in this respect prove useful. In regard to large dense groups of Firs, at least where space permits, vistas of varying character may be opened out, and walks designed, thus very desirably developing effects. In respect of lights and shades amid groups of trees, really beautiful results may be accomplished by having due regard to the circle described by the sun. Nature, indeed, as where the elements have had their will, occasionally takes the matter in hand, and by means of breaks and recesses creates lights and shades for herself. To the foregoing we have to add the variously blended tints of vegetable growths, which constitute, as it were, the very backbone of our arrangements. These tints we must endeavour to study in their darkest as well as lightest modifications, in order to turn them to best account.

Light and shade, in truth, in the arrangement of scenery, are of the very greatest moment, and, after selecting our outline forms, the next best thing to attend to, is, where to introduce them with most advantage. Striking results are sometimes witnessed where the natural beauty of the soil has been made the most of. Thus I remember to have once seen in Derbyshire a spot where the rocks jutted out in bold majestic outlines, in the very midst of fine old forest timber. Such effects, however, are greatly enhanced by the addition of water, as, for example, when sparkling cascades and rushing falls lose themselves in some deep rivulet below.

It is really impossible to have proper lights and shades in scenery, unless we allow to each vegetable growth its adequate natural development. Harmonious combination, however, is matter for deep consideration, and in general it should prove our aim to render our decorative arrangements as little artificial as possible; and if only our laying out and planting be properly managed, we shall never get from them those wearisome impressions which otherwise we are almost certain to experience. Trees should not be inexpressive points, but, united with intermediate objects, should form integral parts of the scene. Single trees, and groups indeed, ought always apparently be forming part of some massive arrangement, thus enhancing the general effect. It is also well to bear in mind the facts to which I have more than once adverted, namely, that dark shades occasion a seeming depression, and show off lighter ones to great advantage; while, on the other hand, light shades impart height, and are a most important adjunct in contributing to distant effects.

That mighty source of light and life, the sun, will prove our best guide in arranging lights and shades, for it is in the sun's power to illumine and transfigure our landscapes in a way which transcends all expression. I have watched many a sunset scene, and many a sunrise, but never was I more filled with admiration than when on one occasion, while at sea, I beheld the sun rise from behind distant hills. On one September morning in 1872, I was passing from Belfast to Fleetwood. There had been a fresh breeze during the night, and the waves rose on every side of the vessel, and dashed along midst clouds of silvery spray. Looking at the remote hills, I presently noticed on their summits a lovely halo, which every moment increased in brightness. Brilliant rays shot athwart the sky, imparting a surpassing beauty, and presently the sun appeared, as if smiling upon the new-born day, and shedding light and gladness on the earth beneath.

CHAPTER III.

BEAUTY.—DIVERSIFICATIONS.

If we would have our arrangements successful, we must never for a moment imagine that we have reached perfection, but, on the contrary, be ever desirous for progress, endeavouring, as it were, to snatch Nature's secrets from her grasp. In decorations, it is well always to be prepared for any pleasing combination of effects that may happen to present itself, for everything should be turned to the best account. It is needful to have the fullest perception of the importance of details, unfettered by narrowness of thought; and to know how to produce powerful effects without coarseness. To give importance to details, however, we must have recourse to contrasts, making these subordinate, indeed, instead of prominent. But of this again.

While the principles of arrangement for decorating the surface of the soil, are—at least in essentials—at once few and simple, they are most multiplex in detail. In these pages I have only noted such as have appeared to me to be of most moment. The following table embodies some of the details :—

$$\text{DIVERSIFICATION OF BEAUTY.} \begin{cases} \text{Feeling} \begin{cases} \text{Love,} \\ \text{Truth,} \end{cases} \\ \text{Observation} \begin{cases} \text{Comparison,} \\ \text{Power,} \\ \text{Contrast,} \\ \text{Unity,} \\ \text{Moderation,} \end{cases} \begin{matrix} \text{Mass or} \\ \text{Infinity} \end{matrix} \begin{matrix} \text{Governed by} \\ \text{Balance,} \\ \text{Proportion,} \\ \text{Harmony,} \end{matrix} \end{cases}$$

all these combining with, and being subordinated to, each other in the production of balance, harmony, and symmetry.

LOVE AND TRUTH.—As a guide for our feelings, we must, if we would originate beautiful conceptions, hold fast by the laws of love and truth in all their grandeur and purity. We must make these two great principles our firm allies, for without them no amount of pains or imagined practical knowledge, no books or worldly store, will suffice to ensure success. Love and truth, indeed, are priceless jewels, short of which nought will avail. Gilpin's love of nature effected, I am well convinced, more good than all his theories. And thus it is that many an old garden, once laid out by loving hands, has a charm and a beauty that are not found in more elaborate arrangements.

These, it has been said, are days of steam; but in beautifying land we can do nothing by steam. Nature's laws and operations, in their vast diversity and grandeur, are in truth far beyond us, and all that we are able to do is to work with her in a loving and reverent spirit. The love which we put into our work, indeed, brings about results at once wondrous and unexpected; for we all, if only we were duly conscious of it, possess an inner might far transcending any outward one —powers and forces which, in too many instances, are, alas! allowed to slumber, but which are capable of development and fruitage in all.

Love and truth are fountains of goodness—fountains whose depths we cannot fathom. Love and truth, indeed, are indissolubly united, for without truth it is impossible to love. Yet the world has sought to draw distinctions, and we hear now and then such expressions as true love, false love, worldly love, spiritual love, as if it were possible, indeed, to draw such lines, and as though love could subsist where truth was not. The first lesson to teach a child is truth: love will yield her lessons in due time. The want of truth it is, which more than anything else, has proved the source of error and misery since the world began. Truth, indeed, is at the root of all success in beautifying land, as in every other art. It is the very philosopher's stone, the test so often sought for—a test which alone can distinguish right from wrong, and, along with love, the first, last best principle for the conduct of life.

Possession is but transitory, and we can have but little of it here below. Therefore it is, that this world's love, used for worldly purposes alone, too often proves untrue. The moment, however, that love assumes a nobler form, it wins respect, and realises power. This we find whenever spiritual ends and objects constitute the battle ground. The face, were it of the humblest peasant, lighted up with love, will possess beauty that the aristocrat might crave. Only witness the change in the face of a child, from trouble to gladness, at the sight of its mother. And thus it is in all stages and alternations of life, from infancy to age. Love, indeed, is the principle that imparts all life. It alters the expression; often changes what is commonplace to absolute beauty. Love is all powerful; it is a Jacob's-ladder which reaches from earth to heaven. It is the very celestial road which conducts us, at once, to paradise; and if only it could be always freed from evil passion, pure love would never taint its object or itself by any untruth. Love and truth must hold together. Love takes away all fear. Love turns toil, even of the heaviest type, into absolute pleasure. It is the vital spark that converts darkness into light. It is the power that turns death into life, for love gives life; it is the lamp of existence, and all earth's treasures were but dross and nothingness without it.

Ruskin has defined truth as "the standard of excellence" in relation to beauty. All, indeed, admire, or affect to admire it, and there is no one who can calmly bear to be dealt with untruthfully. Truth holds up to us the standard of duty, teaches us how to shun temptation, and helps us to guide our feelings aright. As the eye which at one time beams with love may again darken with hatred, so the power of man is great for good as it is great for evil. So, day by day, we continue our upward road, or, it may be, our downward course. And if only we would do any right or true thing, the springs of life must remain unsullied; for without right principles, we can judge of nothing truly. When we yield to evil, thought becomes inaccurate, and judgment misty, for truth and goodness are light and life. Alas! for him who trusts to what is false! The soul can only bring forth that which is in it; it is vain to hope to obtain bread from stones; but when truth guides our steps, we find that it is the very stay and foothold of existence.

CHAPTER IV.

BEAUTY.—COMPARISON.

THE power of feeling fairly transcends all our conceptions, and the scope of observation, from the very unfathomableness of the subject, must remain very far from being complete. After that the spirit is placed in the material of beauty, observation may be made upon parts of its diversification. Beauty is always one, always perfect unity, nothing being wanted to complete its harmony. When a person has learnt a considerable number of facts connected with the beautifying of the earth, his learning acts as a base to his art. He then feels the wants, and supplies the various features, each to the complete satisfaction of itself, and to the whole, until harmony is produced. It is very possible, however, that none can attain unto this feeling without passing through the many steps which are indicated in these pages, and in many more pointing to a similar end, so that the mind may base its actions upon the Love and Truth of all its subjects.

COMPARISON.—In seeking the secrets of Beauty, we shall find the amplest scope in the flowers, which vie with one another in loveliness, and in the leaves as they wave upon the trees, harmonising as they do with each other and with the whole, not in contrast, but in true comparison in all their parts.

Some of the greatest and grandest effects I ever witnessed were produced by a very few variations of the principal forms or colours. To speak of single plants, the *Abies Douglasii* displays its wildness of character in the arrangement of its lights and deep shades. The Elms, north of London, present rounded and undulating forms, replete with amenity and grace. Any one, indeed, who interrogates Nature will find that she produces results the most marvellous in mountain scenery, in the formation of her ground-work, by means which, if analysed, are found to reside in infinity of details, but she makes very few changes in the principles of form. Much by means of little; *beaucoup avec peu* is in fact our motto. Sometimes, indeed, results the most important may be obtained from but a few minute changes in the curvature of the line.

The word "comparison" is perhaps the best I can make use of in order to convey a sense of the general feeling which I desire to express. Plants should preserve their individual character, in due subordination with the general arrangement, and not be jumbled up unmeaningly together to the ruin of all true effect. If, indeed, plants had less beauty than they actually possess, still it must wound the soul of the observer to witness the harshness and inconsequence with which they are too often treated. Contrast, when rightly used, is in truth the source of developing great beauty ; but, if we neglect the comparison of our subject, the results must prove unsatisfactory. In contemplating some scene of natural beauty with its refined foreground, dying away into infinity, the soul is, as it were, filled up with, and steeped in its harmony. No work in which the principles of harmony are violated can further the true interests of art, while those which instil a just feeling of unison with the subject must necessarily do good. It is easy to find examples. Scenery, indeed, must be true to Nature and effect, else the results cannot possibly prove satisfactory.

Beauty is plastic, for as the potter fashions his clay, for honour or dishonour, so it rests with the arranger of scenery to render it beautiful or otherwise. The very noblest objects of earth—to wit, man himself— become hateful or pleasing according to the way in which they are handled. We are, in a sense, the makers of beauty around us, and we are bound to treat with distinction the materials which have been confided to us. The individual who might become an object of imitation and admiration, will be consigned by evil passions to darkness and disgrace. Even the worst of men, I believe, will look back with a regretful pleasure to the purer impulses of the past, though they cannot hope to revel in the pleasant memories which feed the soul of the good man, and which shine in his life as the very stars of heaven for ever.

Beauty ministers to the heart of man, and affects the spirit in a manner that surpasses comprehension. Beauty nurtures the soul. Beauty is unfathomable. And yet I have no hesitation in asserting that it is possible for us so to arrange our landscapes that each new day shall reveal to the attentive observer a fresh loveliness. Nevertheless, how often do we see even large gardens laid out in such fashion that a very short time, indeed, suffices to behold all that is worth beholding. In general, it is well not to make use of too strong contrasts, but gently to modify, without violence, the characters of each several scene.

Whatever the arena of our arrangement in decorative landscape may be, the first thing to do is to be guided by correct principles as regards form and colour, and then subordinate our materials to these. How often are flower beds or trees so placed that, though beautiful in themselves, they are quite out of keeping with their surroundings, through some mistaken desire to show off, to the great injury and prejudice of the general effect? It is quite indispensable, indeed, that a scene should preserve its true character—in fact, this is one of the chief difficulties with which amateur gardeners have to deal. They wish to compass pleasing effects without, apparently, giving a thought to comparison with the subjects around. To attempt the laying out of grounds, without some general knowledge, is an undertaking worse than useless. Book-lore alone cannot possibly supply the place of practical knowledge. Whatever may be the matter in hand, well defined principles should always be kept in view. Comparison, when properly handled, yields very desirable results. The sharp contours of rocks, the easy flowing undulations of level country, the straight lines of buildings—all afford elements of beauty when the arrangement is kept true to their principle. Man (for such is his complex nature) ever seeks for and desires something new; and the most lovely scene palls when constantly repeated. It is needful, therefore, to give as great variety as possible, consistently with good taste, in our landscape decorations. Thus, a wood or a shrubbery, though unimportant in itself, may, by allowing the mind to repose before bringing forward new beauties, often be turned to excellent account.

Whatever arrangements, then, we may decide upon, there must, as I said before, be some well-grounded principle in respect of the direction of each. Minor effects should so harmonise as to yield scope in other beauties as well as their own. For example, if we try to enhance the beauty of the sloping sward or fulfil to satisfaction the ground outlines of groups, by anything except a curve in the ground or outlines of the figures—say by a tree—we shall soon find how useless is the attempt. Curves in ground need other curves to balance them, and shrubs other shrubs. Thus the effect of each line of sight must receive a just proportion of its own effects, to give satisfaction in the details and general result, all bearing a true relation to each other. Efforts are sometimes made to imitate Nature in her more romantic moods, such as placing mock rocks contiguous to artificial ponds, but such attempts are rarely attended with desirable results. It is frequently, I admit, expedient to have recourse to lines of much straightness in their general effects to compare with water, when we have not enough; but only a sheer want of natural knowledge can ever lead any one to introduce rocks in places which are eminently unsuited for them. Plant life, in its various aspects, will give comparisons enough to suit level scenery, water inclusive, without having recourse to meaningless heaps of stone. Where, however, Nature herself lends aid in the way of rocks and otherwise, they can and ought to be turned to good account.

Beautiful scenery is impossible when violent contrasts and incongruous details are made use of for the principles of arrangement. Every natural object, when rightly placed in comparison, contributes to the harmony of the general result. Many, indeed, are the avenues that conduct to the beautiful; and the tasteful artistic arranger has the power to impart infinite satisfaction by means of well-devised judicious arrangements; otherwise violent contrasts simply defeat their purposes, and mar the beauty of the whole.

The principle is virtually one and the same whether large or small pieces of ground have to undergo decoration. Frequently, the most charming effects have resulted in limited spots which, once planted, are then simply left for long years to Nature's fostering care. Cases of this kind, however, must obviously prove less satisfactory than results worked out by earnest thought and care. It is altogether a mistake to mass one species of growth in one place without making any provision for suitable surroundings. Nature, indeed, must ever prove our great exemplar; with her we must ever work and strive, and, when once this great fact shall be thoroughly recognised and acted on, consequences more beautiful and striking than most persons have ventured to imagine must ensue.

When we look on some flat, unvarying surface, how little admiration does it provoke. But only introduce a few diversities of form, for comparison, and lay down the proper plants, whereupon the monotony disappears. It is quite an error to lavish indiscriminate admiration on one colour to the disparagement of another Each varying form or hue, when associated with its fitting accessories, is beautiful in turn. It is, indeed, natural enough for people to have their favourite lines and outlines; but it is when these are brought too prominently forward, that ill effects ensue. For tints and outlines, when properly compared and adjusted, gain fresh beauty, and impart an ever-renewed satisfaction.

POWER.—Beauty always displays a power to do something—and we must not do less—upon our landscapes. Trees, in all their varying forms, the outlines of the soil, colours with their brilliant splendour, their mysterious lights and shades, will aid us much in respect of this. Certain trees best display their contour quite close to the summit of their stems. What are termed breaks also often afford satisfactory results. Trees that rise much above the general line of vegetation enhance the bold outline of the whole. Every beauty is complete in something, as the outlines of the human body, the contour of a tree, or the undulations of a mountain—they all accomplish something, and this doing something, must be observed in arranging all scenery by taking in the details of its parts, the character or characters, and arranging their form, or what might be called binding, the heights, hollows, recesses, and promontories, &c.; this act I venture to call power. In judging the forms for the power to accomplish, the land, the surrounding, and the object arranged for, will give a base for the detail and general outlines of the scenery. This act of power in beauty is admirably shown in tree life.

CONTRAST.—Opposite colours or forms, in particular scenes, attract the least observant, and lead the eye to combinations which otherwise might have remained unnoticed for ever. Sometimes the position of a single curious plant may be so adjusted as to afford the beholder a spectacle of arrangements, far surpassing in effect the plant itself in their capacity to yield enjoyment. Colour, in most cases, furnishes a potent attraction—a small amount of gold, for instance, accomplishes much. But more of this again. A sufficient knowledge of the proper use of contrast is not, in truth, to be acquired without prolonged and earnest study. Without this we may indeed compass results, but they will be more surprising than satisfactory.

Contrast has something to do with the development of beauty, but is not beauty itself. For instance, a scene composed of upright growing plants can be developed by plants of another form, but these must not destroy the principal character of the upright forms; on the contrary, assist their development. Contrast may also be used as a guide to scenery: it is excitement without satisfaction.

UNION.—It is an absolute necessity that a happy state of unison should subsist in respect of the different portions of our scenery, multiplying, indeed, the harmony and symmetry which each vegetable growth displays in all its parts. Would we only fittingly combine the various scenes which our landscapes are to present, it must be accomplished by means of gentle gradations both in outline and colour. Thus, nigh a dwelling-house of some extent, we should be governed in our operations by the lines displayed in the house itself. Wild scenery ought not to come up to our very doors, nor the waving and sometimes rugged outlines of the forest prove the limitaries of grand mansions. It is well to have some intermediate character of lines to give union— for example, the *Cedrus Lebani*, in all its natural majesty, will not, when in contiguity, prove incongruous. It will, indeed, very greatly embellish straight lines and level surfaces, and prepare the observer for yet greater diversity of forms.

In order that a visible harmony may subsist in our landscapes, it is needful that each growth should be severally adapted to the character of the soil, so that the efforts of art should tend always to enhance the conditions of Nature. In the more immediate vicinity of mansions, the trees, shrubs, and carpeting plants employed ought to prove duly decorative. It will never do, for example, for a palace to seem lost as it were in a wood. Often the arrangements in flower-gardens attached to places of importance may appear poor in detail, and yet prove right in principle from their subordination to the mansion, any deficiency in artificial outline being amply compensated for in the surrounding natural effects of hill and dale, where every character may receive its own satisfaction. Water, also, when present, exercises quite a magic power in uniting and harmonising the various component parts of scenery.

Some forms of architecture—Gothic structures, for example— yield, or appear to yield, much assistance in decoration. Their irregular outlines, lights and shades, seem to meet us half way in our efforts. Italian architecture, and gardens also, are admirably adjusted to each other. Turrets, ornamental roofs, and campaniles, are of very great use, and take away the baldness and platitude inseparable from certain styles. These and other matters will aid us very materially in enhancing decorations contiguous to dwelling-houses, as well as tend to render gardens themselves arenas of beauty.

The vistas of pleasure grounds must so unite with natural scenery that the spectator may not all at once discern the dividing line. Plantations ought never to terminate abruptly, but gracefully and gradually blend with the boundaries of the landscape, thus effecting an approximate union between Nature's handiwork and our own. We must in every respect endeavour so to apportion our scenery in its details that a proper adjustment shall subsist in every part. For, as Ruskin states, and as I believe most firmly, moderation is the girdle of beauty.

Thus beauty is composed of many elements, more, indeed, than I can pretend to know. The particulars which I have here given, however, appear to me to be founded on Nature and on truth. When we survey a stately tree, for example, how many charms, on near inspection, will be discernible. The leaves and flowers, if the plant be in flower, may seem alike, but in reality are not so; each and every one differs, on examination, from its neighbour. Stand a little further off, and the contour of its masses will appear, on casual view, to be the same, and yet they vary much. A like diversity will also prove observable in outlines powerfully contributing to the general effect, and imparting unity, amenity, and dignity to the whole.

There is no better way for giving unity of character to scenery, than that observed in the works of Nature. In her outlines the unity of the different parts of a character is produced by the general curve or outlines, possessing another curve, or more, within themselves.

The regular curvature of the first appearance exhibits, upon closer observation, many of these miniature curves, all assisting to form the larger outlines; thus Nature unites different parts into one character.

Nature, again, in her calm scenes, unites one character to another by gentle gradations, entwining each other in the line of union, so that you are never sure where one commences and the other ends, as masses of vegetation group into each other.

Nature also, in land of great diversification, unites various characters by sudden union, by each character running in bold, sharp promontories into each other, and the vigour of this union is in perfect keeping with the natural effects. Thus Nature uses curvature for everything, but it is always suitable, according to the beauty it has to build, and the arrangements of man cannot do better than follow Nature. (See ground plan in PLATE 2.)

These three natural ways of union should be properly studied before attempting any union of the parts or characters of scenery.

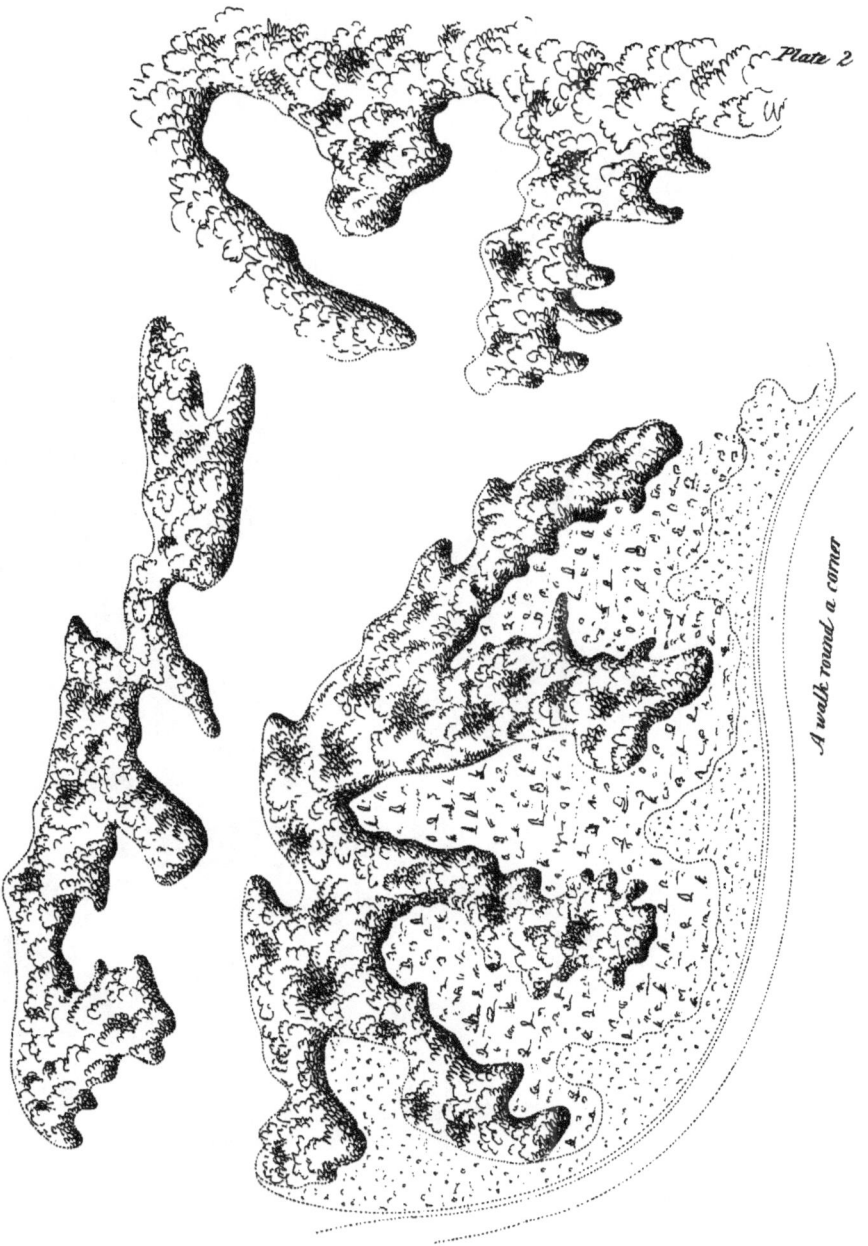

Plate 2

A walk round a corner

CHAPTER V.

GENERAL OBSERVATION FOR BEAUTY.

WHATEVER objects are displayed they must be so ordered that they shall yield the greatest possible amount of satisfaction to the beholder. Flowers will prove in this respect our firmest allies ; for the smallest and apparently most insignificant forms, when viewed alone, are beautiful when grouped together. Effects may be broadly divided into proximate and remote—those which blend immediately together, and those which extend into the distance, and continue to smile upon us though afar off. These things, in fact, are needful to the production of real and lasting results. Proper distances, too, ought to be observed in arranging subjects according to the character of the objects treated. Lines are to be preferred which conduct to the greatest variety of desirable effects, particularly when aided by the undulations of the soil. These lines, indeed, are susceptible of almost infinite variety.

The lines of infinity and mass, as represented in PLATE 3, command the material into order for use in forming the various elements of beauty. The lines curving towards the reader, as shown in PLATE 3, give those which will present the most material to the mind at once. The perspective lines furnish those which will give the most thought to the mind—observe these are curves. These two principles form the basis in all the arrangement of scenery characters. Their effects are first to be noticed, and to be laid down in proportion; moreover, they will give place to all other lesser forms in such accordance as is required for vegetation. Those who have not noticed these lines before to guide them in planting vegetation, will be surprised at the command they give when used. They confer full power to create any feelings of which the land is capable, in accordance with the character of the position, each site exhibiting its own particular effect.

These lines should be used according to the natural formation of the ground to be beautified. No straining should be attempted to give more than is natural to the place, in just proportion of feelings, for there are plants of infinite characters which will beautify either small or large effects. Thus, the line curving concavely, in all its various forms, towards the individual, gives material to the mind, and the line curving convexly, or from, gives him occasion for thought. Thus the beauty of each character, in its development, gives either its material or thought to the mind.

In arranging vegetable growths it is needful that a proper balance should subsist throughout. In gardens arranged on geometrical principles it is not unusual to repeat the same subject at equal distances. But Nature's scenery varies ever, and yet preserves the truest balance. Among other treatises abounding with desirable suggestions, I would earnestly urge the careful study of the pages of Mr. Ruskin's "Modern Painters" respecting union.

Balance in arranging scenery is the art of giving each effect, small or large, its proper share of thought, so as to produce, in its development, a perfect whole, as a scene of wild masses of rounding curvature of outlines might be succeeded by sharp bold outlines, thus giving finish, as it were, by the first thought and preparing it for the next effects of scenery, taking the sweeping curves of undulations in its formations. Balance is giving these effects in proper feeling, quantity, and number, according to the place. The only law I am acquainted with which is useful as a guide is the one necessary for everything— viz., you must have a principle to work out, so that although each effect is perfect, still its feeling must give assistance to the proper balance of the whole effects of, say the valley which you are arranging. I have often been greatly pleased with the balance of the massing of trees building up their outlines, and still each mass perfect in itself. Everything must have a true balance.

Harmony is the very foundation and completion of beauty, and whatever may be our object, to establish harmony should ever be borne in mind, while every effect must be complete in itself, and in harmony with others. Its light must guide our steps. Efforts to produce great results by means of mere contrasts, instead of a union of effects, are vain and futile, and cannot be attended with success. In landscapes where the trees have reached a certain maturity of growth, and where Nature for a period has wrought her own will, scenes the most charming may be witnessed.

Plate 3

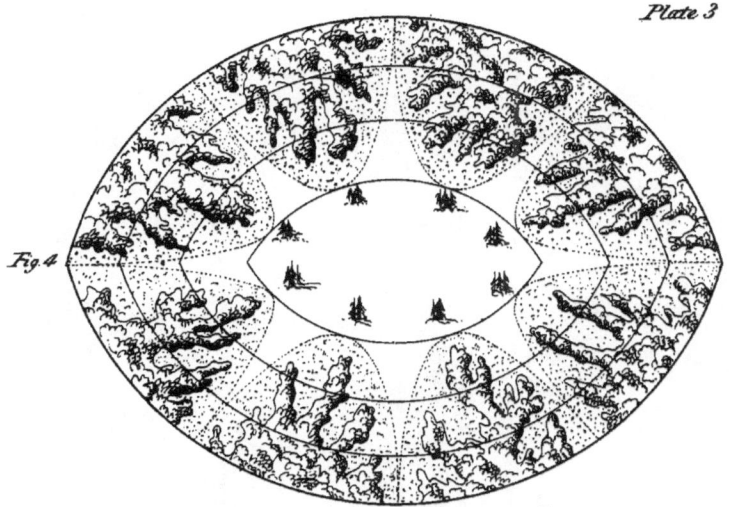

Fig. 4

Laws of distance for Massing and Extent.

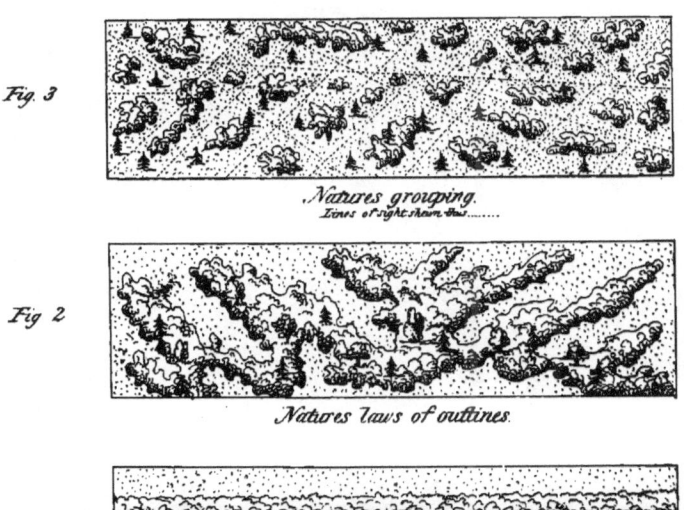

Fig. 3

Natures grouping.
Lines of sight shewn thus........

Fig. 2

Natures laws of outlines.

Fig. 1

Outlines producing the least effect.

In the structure of rocks in mountainous districts a visible harmony is often subsistent. Details may seem to vary, but, on examination, they are in essentials the same. The smaller outlines pass into larger, until at length the eye rests on the battlemented summits, where Nature's mighty handiwork inspires thoughts of awe and grandeur. Mountainous tracts, indeed, exhibit countless varieties of outline, masses differing very greatly from those of more level lands ; while again the latter are distinguished by undulations and curves peculiar to themselves.

To follow Nature should be our constant care, and yet how often is Nature set at naught! The boundaries of gardens are crowded with forest trees, Beeches, for instance, serving as a basis. Then perhaps a few Coniferæ are dotted here and there, a Purple Beech or two, each presenting contrasts to the rest. And yet the worse and more violent the contrast the more are we expected to admire scenes of this description, where Nature's example is turned to no account, disgusting people of taste, and perhaps leading in many instances to some opposite extreme. When it is found desirable to use masses of Purple Beech in order to impart depth to clumps of deciduous trees, golden-hued plants, or others similar, enhance the general effect. The Purple Beech, indeed, is well adapted for foregrounds, but does not readily admit of being dotted over the landscape.

Harmony, both in form and colour, is of the very greatest importance ; no successful arrangement is possible without it. It is needful, indeed, to insist thoroughly on this point, for scenery is ruined where it fails to be attended to. In respect of colour, purple harmonises admirably with gold, serving to bring it near, but white and gold together seldom please. Colour, in truth, impresses every one. Some, indeed, appear as if satisfied with it alone, but minds of a higher order, who seek for the living substance, can alone be contented with the harmony that underlies all things.

Harmony is a feeling produced by the completion of everything to each other's satisfaction, not one equal to another, but everything taking a proper place in the formation of the scenery, thus producing results that give beauty.

Book II.—LAW OF ORDER.

CHAPTER I.

LINES OF SIGHT.

In regard of diversity in form and colour, it will prove needful to lay down a few general principles with a view to avoid confusion. These I would sum up under the following seven heads—to wit, *Lines of Sight, Lines of Distance, Place, Sites, Character, Outlines, and Time.*

To order scenery is like beginning to transform the world, to found a dwelling, not merely for the body, but for the soul also. Many things have to be considered at once for beauty and for use. We have first to devise a method of procedure, and then to adapt it to the circumstances of the case, and also to the localities with which we have to deal.

Lines of Sight.—To impart a due sense of satisfaction in scenery, three sizes of vegetable growths will prove desirable. First come the plants that are to carpet the soil, occupying, as it were, the first line; secondly, shrubs, so termed, holding a sort of intermediate position, rising out of the ground line; and, thirdly, trees, imparting the greatest effects, rising above all. We cannot, indeed, make any quite arbitrary divisions in this matter, since in all the productions of Nature the most beautiful union obtains. In Nature, indeed, we see variety of form harmoniously disposed, every feature lovely. Whether viewed as part or as a whole, the ground undulates so as to impart an aspect of life and warmth. It is only in gardens that we find surfaces which the hand of man has striven to render uninteresting, the levelled soil being raked into finest dust, and the lines of sight held of little or no account, leading to results often the very reverse of pleasing.

The eye can only take in well one impression at a time, though perhaps some trees—pyramidal specimens of the Fir tribe, for example—

yield many complex effects within themselves, still, when the general outlines are viewed you do not take in any other beauty. To a student of Nature the amount and variety of vegetation that now almost everywhere abounds, furnishes a never-failing, ever-increasing source of satisfaction and information. Food for thought, in truth, everywhere abounds in those wonderful growths that so beautify the world, each in itself proving a miracle of loveliness, wondrously adapted to the situation it has to occupy.

The study of climate is needful in order to determine what plants are likely to suit, these varying extremely in structure, conditions, and requirements. I have, for instance, seen the Fuchsia, which in most parts of the centre of England is killed down to the ground in winter, actually thirty-five feet high in Ireland. The irregular outlines are the only ones which give place for lines of sight to good results in harmony. In these we may often, with much advantage, have many varieties yielding different effects at different periods of the year, even in carpeting plants alone. For example, we may have the early foliage of the Lupins, then flowers, Delphiniums, or late Asters, &c., all grouping in the foreground masses. These when they cover a space of ground, for a long time produce good results. (See PLATE 2 and others).

CHAPTER II.

LINES OF DISTANCES.

THE selection of proper sites in gardens is a more important matter than has been commonly supposed. It has often been said that a garden ought not to be seen in all its parts at once, but it is not always that the whole bearing of this sentence is considered. Our landscapes greatly depend for effect on proper distances being observed. For example, as regards general effects, a large subject requires to be placed at a greater distance than a small one when its own greatest effect is wanted : just as to display fitly the beauty of extensive groups of flowers we must choose a situation more remote than for blossoms of tiny growth. The lines of sight should unite according to the laws of union.

As regards our lines of sight, it behoves us to consider how we are to accommodate them to the various distances, inasmuch as objects vary extremely as we approach or recede from them. The lovely outlines of leaves and flowers are not visible from a distance. Mass and outline, in that case, impress us most. Quiet groups of trees, forming parts of other vegetation, soften best the contour of remote hills. It is not commonly either practicable or desirable to extend gardens to the limits of the horizon. In any and every case, however, we can observe the proper distances in laying out carpeting plants and deciduous and permanent shrubs and trees, so as to combine the whole scenes together for good general results.

A due regard to the laws of perspective will give an apparent increase to our landscape. (See PLATE 3, Figure 4, which will explain this better than words, also the lines of distances, &c.) In decoration it is of absolute importance that very great care should be taken as regards the treatment of distant views, for these impart very powerful effects. Numerous facilities, indeed, always abound for diversifying projections and recesses. (See PLATE 4, Page 45, as referring to avenues.) Persons accustomed to level ground do not at once realise the amount

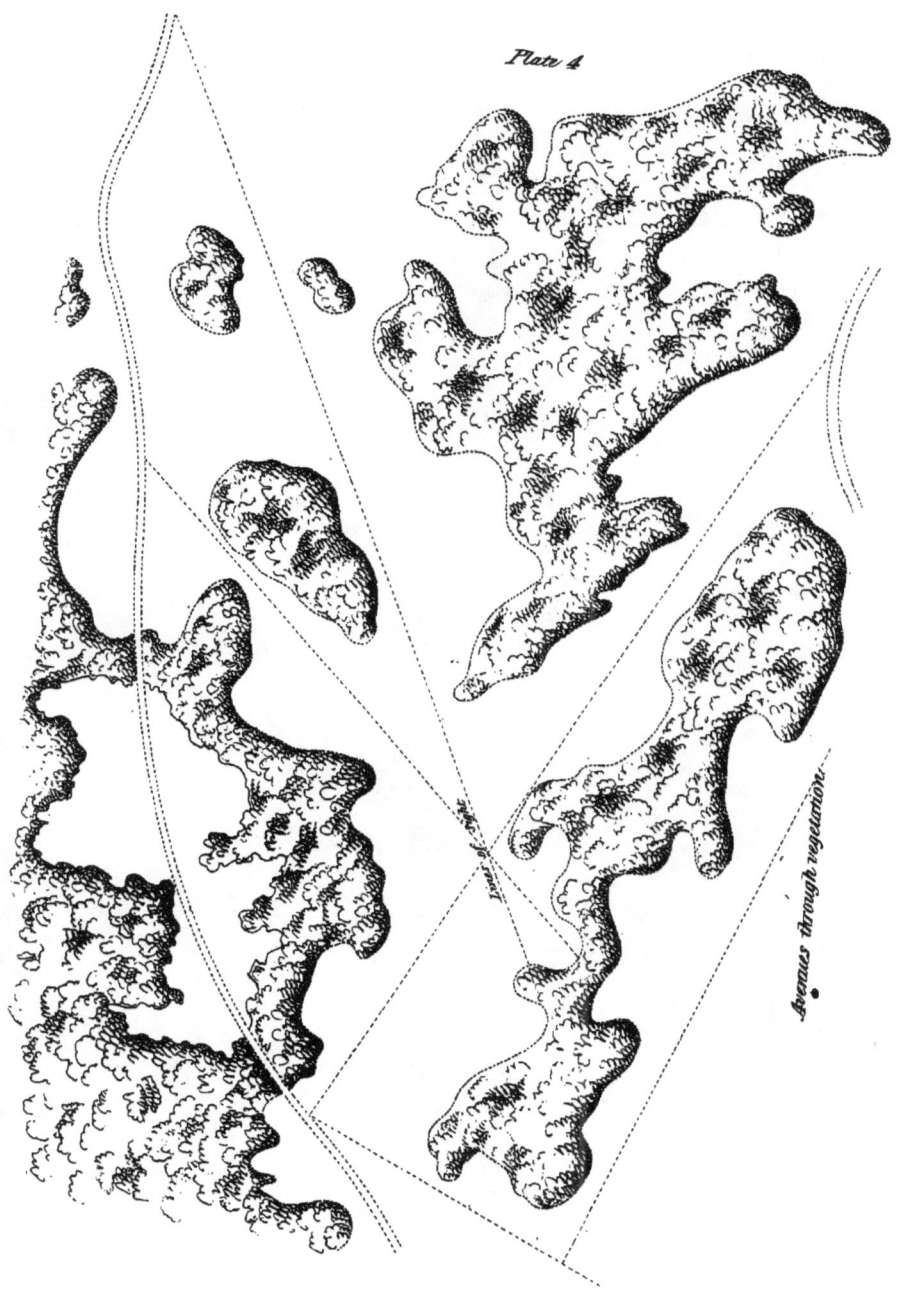

Plate 4

of surface contained in a hill, being quite unaware of the quantity of materials as thus submitted to inspection.

In surveying falling ground, the lines of sight appear to recede, conveying a sense of distance, much being unseen that would be otherwise plainly visible. In Nature, where there is rising there is always falling ground. Nature's laws are ever true, and, if we would but conform to them, our gardens would present beauties which they now but rarely display. When all the lines of sight have their proper proportion, it is impossible for the distances to be wrong.

In extended landscapes—for example, in hilly districts and other favoured spots—the vegetation, of whatever character, will be a foreground to the scenery. Then there is a mid-ground, and perhaps, further on, the outlines of distant mountains. Great effects may often be compassed by masses of forest scenery on the higher grounds. This is one reason for the delightful aspect of the grounds in Tollymore Park, in the County of Down. Here the woods are in truest harmony with the mountains beyond. The effects at the entrance of the park, indeed, I have seldom, if ever, seen equalled. It is worthy to be the portal of a castle dwelt in by heroes such as those of whom Homer sings.

CHAPTER III.

PLACE.

NOTHING can well be of greater moment than the selection of a good site, or that of rendering a site already selected suitable for the objects meant to occupy it. However beautiful materials may prove in themselves, unless they are properly placed they will fail to display their attractions. The first things to be considered are the surroundings. These must be in proper keeping, whether they are meant to encircle flower-beds or extended landscapes. In every case they very powerfully govern effects. How often do people hold forth about the best method of laying out a garden without ever properly taking into account the boundaries thereof, thus, occasionally, being led into very serious mistakes. Then let our arrangements be what they may, the effects will greatly depend on the surroundings, and ought to be carried out in strict accordance with them.

It is owing to faulty arrangements that so many fine varieties of plants, plants quite within our reach, are not more frequently met with. Were natural arrangements only properly adjusted, space might readily be found for growths well adapted to embellish and adorn, and which are now overlooked and neglected. How many spots are there where scenery might be beautiful, and yet where but a few objects either interest or please. Often and often places are cut up so as to satisfy some prevailing whim or fashion, instead of being laid out so as to develop each possible beauty of form and colour.

Effects may be either general or particular. Objects very pleasing and suitable in one place, may prove quite harsh and unsuitable in another. Instances of this unhappily are not wanting. The common Beech, more especially in small gardens, mars the effect of everything about it; it has not sufficient space for development, and yet how often may one gaze for hours together, on some hill side, on beechen foliage that is perfectly enchanting, untouched by art: Nature's hand alone has clothed it with tenderness and beauty.

Stately artificial decorations may beseem the neighbourhood of a mansion ; but the more Nature is followed in the arrangement of our vegetation, &c., the more attractive our landscapes will prove. Sir Walter Scott, in a few lines in his "St. Ronan's Well," refers to the different conditions of feeling in which we may set about the decoration of land. Speaking of one of his characters, he says :—"Winter-blossom's taste was rather of the technical kind. It neither warmed the heart nor elevated the feelings." Whether our arrangements be natural or artificial, it will be always in our power to approximate them more or less to what is beautiful and elevating.

To lay out scenery so as to compass any approach to perfection will demand both careful thought and practice. We have to give the greatest possible satisfaction to the beholder. In colour certain lines being present, yield most pleasure. When they follow a succession, first gold, then purple, then silver, lastly blue is desirable.

All agree in acknowledging how enjoyable is scenery where one is half lost in the green mazes of a thicket, and when some lovely prospect discloses itself, or again, when our path is shut in by rocks. Minor effects enhance greater ones, impart increased beauty to all. Pauses, so to speak, are very desirable, not only in garden scenery, but in Nature as well. But numerous facilities exist for strengthening our outlines and enhancing the general effect. The general outlines govern place, therefore the outlines of every scene should be made suitable for the details to be worked out therein.

CHAPTER IV.

SITES.

In most localities, as is well known, there are certain points from which the scenery can be better discerned than from others. These, when they do not previously subsist, can be constructed artificially, either by raising the ground, or by opening out vistas. Spots of this kind are generally termed sites, the best, for the most part, being selected for the house, while the rest are of great advantage in respect of decoration. It is desirable to give the scenery therefrom its guides, so as to make the most of it. They serve, indeed, as a species of landmark, and make us acquainted with the general effects. Sites should afford a suitable foreground to the distant effects, but it may also prove desirable to use some object or objects, small or large, according to circumstances, so as to attract the attention of the beholders, these serving as guides and indices to the scene. The Golden Yew, or the *Aucuba*, are well adapted for this purpose; otherwise some growth where the form and colour suit. In other respects, it is not requisite that the objects adverted to should occupy much space, or evince a too conspicuous elevation. It is best that they should be of medium size, so as naturally to attract the eye, not occupying the attention too much, but subserving the scene by introducing us to it.

It will be needful for guides to be, as it were, in unison with the scene; therefore, we shall have to select them with a view to permanent effect. No pleasure grounds, indeed, will prove complete without objects of this kind—not all displaying one and the same line or outline, but varying according to the landscape.

It is a material drawback to both pleasure and comfort when we are obliged to have recourse to some one to point out beauties that should reveal themselves unsought. Either they are not worth seeing, or else our powers of observation are at fault.

Walks, whether of grass, gravel, or other material, should be constructed near sites calling for admiration. Not unfrequently, simple objects guiding the sight, such as sundials, should be placed; attractive seats, retreats, and the like will serve the same purpose. In other respects, we may, in the more artistic portion of our grounds, have recourse to statuary or vases with this intent. In choosing sites beware of compulsion in feelings being given to the effects; for instance, it will not prove advantageous to select a more prominent situation than is actually necessary to develop our effects to the sight. Sometimes, indeed, faulty objects bearing no true relation to the scene are brought to the front. This, and undue prominence of the objects selected, impart a forced instead of a natural and pleasing expression to the landscape. It is quite needful that our displays should not lose any of their breadth or effect.

We must avoid everything forced and unnatural, as it will but serve to impart an expression of harshness and discordancy. There must be some very strong reason for doing so, ere we think of placing objects so as directly to challenge attention. Another very objectionable procedure is to construct recesses at right angles to walks or sites, so that they cannot be seen without turning the head. These methods are but too often adopted in decoration, leading to results the very reverse of pleasing. A golden mean, when attainable, avoiding all extremes, will prove best suited to our purposes in the long run. It is quite needful that we should be enabled to behold some more or less considerable portion of the scenery, without having to turn the head from the position which we may happen to occupy. (See Roads in PLATES 2 and 4, how they curve to show the views without exposing them.)

Decorations ought not to be obtrusive. Subjects should not come into view whether we wish to see them or not, nor should an arrangement be such as to strain the sight to look at it. Nature, indeed, furnishes means which will enable us to avoid all such absurd and awkward extremes. Sites from which good effects are visible are justifiable sources for solicitude, but those from which bad effects, or objects not in character with the scene are discernible, should likewise be matter of attention, with a view to avoid them. And yet, unhappily, such as these are everywhere to be witnessed. Large level plots of grass, often at considerable cost, perhaps, disclose views at once pleasing and displeasing. This must be seen to. All reasonable accessories are desirable, but nothing in the treatment to impair or mar the general effect. It is the ground itself, and the vegetation which it is calculated to display, that should be our care ; whereas this is forgotten when walks are twisted here and there as though they alone were worthy of attention or inspection. When decoration is fittingly carried out, such results will never ensue. By means of a proper arrangement, we are enabled to embellish such spots with miniature carpeting plants, trees, or shrubs, each according to the requirements of the individual case. (See PLATE 5).

Walks, though not perhaps beautiful in themselves, are made to subserve very important purposes. Now boldly sweeping, again in simple curves, they may be varied almost to infinity. By means of observation and judicious care we shall find out when lines intercept the scenery, and when they harmonise with it, as they ought always to do. Some curves consort with the scenery, while others prove adverse. On the whole, our ground, the walks which conduct through it, and the plantations which diversify it, should all be arranged so as to conduce to desirable and harmonious results.

In respect of paths, there are, so to speak, two kinds, one to subserve ordinary useful purposes, the other to aid our efforts in the development of what is beautiful. Each should be arranged in strict subservience to the object for which it is designed. Roads constructed for use should have no meaningless bends or turns, whereas, too often, they may be seen winding in a sort of corkscrew fashion, now this way and now that, in approaching a house. This is done with a false view to make a good carriage drive.

To give visitors, however, the greatest amount of trouble in coming to your dwelling, is hardly desirable. To violate good taste can never make any place look beautiful, which is the reason commonly alleged for the commission of such blunders. Another mistake, often attempted, is to make roads seem the principal attraction, instead of simply ministering to the beauty of the place. They should, in fact, aim at no higher object than does a piece of canvas in the matter of a picture.

Walks are perfect eyesores when they come right across the foreground of an otherwise good piece of scenery. When a walk proves absolutely requisite, in a case like this, it will be best to let it go in

Plate 5.

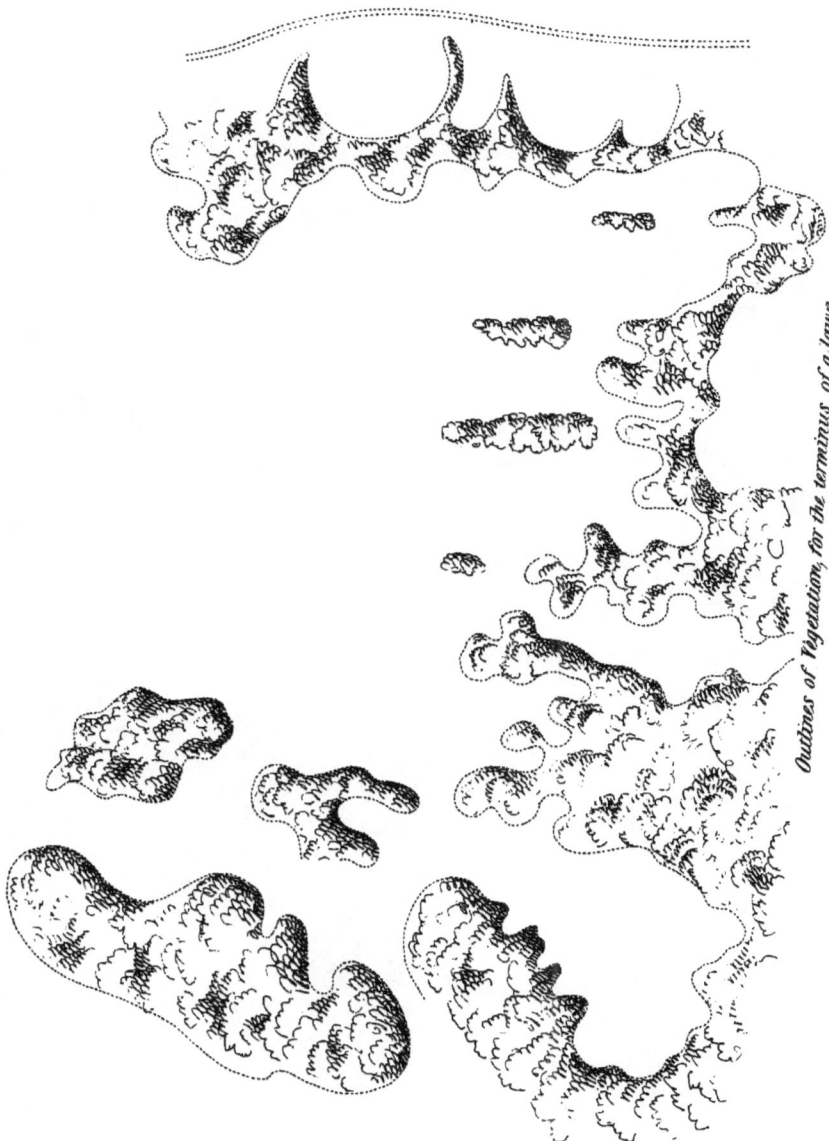

Outlines of Vegetation, for the terminus of a lawn.

the direction of the scenery, and appear as it were to assimilate with it. In other respects, walks and drives are important in any vicinity, but people ought to study the objects for which they are intended ; the natural ways of the place will then blend fittingly with the surrounding scenery. Near a mansion straight walks are more or less advantageous, but whenever the eye once rests on green grass from the windows, straight walks are afterwards unnecessary ; and when they cut straight across the lawn from the windows, I must pronounce straight walks to be radically wrong.

Roads should be constructed, indeed, in order to set off the beauties of a place, and for convenience of approach. It will be needful, with a view to a good foundation, that there should be some hard material, but this rule is not always carried out. Often, in truth, roads are left in so very unsatisfactory a state that they have to be re-made. It will always prove best and cheapest in the end that the construction should be firm and durable, so as to meet even more stress than will be required in the general traffic. Sometimes it will be expedient to have recourse to a basis of concrete, which is more durable and satisfactory than is commonly imagined.

In cases where roads running nigh pleasure grounds might prove too noisy, it will make a great difference in this respect if only timber be employed in their construction. Not very unfrequently we have in our grounds walks that are dry, firm, and would be comfortable to tread upon, except from their being constructed too high in the centre. This very much detracts from their utility, and renders them unsightly when taken in connection with the soil on each side. The level of the path should be about half an inch below the edge of the grass or other material, while the centre should be on the level of the grass, assuming in this case that each side has the same elevation. If these principles be properly carried out there will always be a sufficient fall to remove the surface water in ordinary cases from a properly formed path.

Paths are generally made with parallel sides, whether they come under the designation of high roads, roads for private use, or as yielding access to scenic or other beauties. They should, however, be adapted to their surroundings, and otherwise prove available at all periods of the year. Sometimes, indeed, the parallel lines may be altered so as to give place to figures or statues, and to other suitable decorations.

Near buildings a straight path or promenade will be often preferable (but the effect is by no means so suitable in other places as when we are enabled to have recourse to curved lines), serving as a sort of break or rest between a building and the natural scenery about, or acting as a base to the building in some cases. They are also convenient for taking exercise upon, being commonly within easy reach of shelter during precarious or unsettled weather. Walks should be enlivened by suitable growths or other permanent effects. Climbing plants in this way often prove most serviceable.

It is a source of annoyance when, perhaps in the midst of some lovely scenery, one comes across some gathering of rubbish in our walks. Such unsightly objects should never be permitted. By the judicious employment of earthen banks and planting, we shall always be able to dispose of them. Nothing, in fact, can justify their appearance. The construction of a good rubbish hole, at a time when you are making alterations for which soil is needed, is a very simple matter. Indeed, the materials taken from the hole itself can be so arranged as to conceal everything objectionable.

Paths have to sustain many a footfall. The little child totters along, plucking the flowers as it goes; the maiden trips, hardly touching the ground as she passes; the soldier treads as though he would impress the very stone; and the man of care traverses them he hardly knows when or how. Paths, in fact, like everything else, must be, as much as possible, in unison with the general scenery. Our scenery, in fact, must be harmonious, or it is nothing. It will never otherwise approximate, even to a limited extent, to the beautiful in Nature. Sometimes, from a wish to display objects to advantage, as, for instance, specimen trees near a walk, it may happen that the landscape itself is forgotten. This is only exceptionally permissible, as, for example, in the case of adjuncts to buildings, the judicious disposition of flower-beds, and the like.

Walks should be ordered so as to yield a good prospect, one that shall prove worthy of the surroundings. They are not set up for their own sake, but in subordination to this alone. This premised, every sort of display is admissible that shall not prove incongruous.

The rule is alike important, whether we have regard to general scenery or only to particular effects, as of rocks, water, hills, dales, and the like. Walks that mar instead of enhancing the outlook, must really not be thought of. In other respects, walks and passages from place to place, hedges and railway sidings, might be turned to vastly greater account than they are. Spaces now left almost wholly vacant might be made to yield a prodigious outcome. Thousands and tens of thousands of pounds are yearly expended in the importation of fruits which are truly valuable and desirable, but which, for the most part, might, with the utmost facility and economy, be produced at home. At this very moment, there subsists along one of the railways leading from Ostend, fifteen miles of Espalier Pear Trees on one side, and fifteen miles on the other, making thirty miles in all. There is not an available corner in Switzerland in which Cherry Trees or other fruit-bearing trees are not planted. It is the same in very many parts of Europe, and Asia Minor as well. Were our otherwise waste and unoccupied spaces planted with Plums, Apples, Nuts, and Cherry Trees, Potherbs, and Culinary Plants of various kinds, it would prove an infinite advantage to the community, and one not less profitable than delightful. Nothing surprises foreigners who come over here more than the paucity of fruit-bearing trees in England, Scotland, and Ireland; nor is there, indeed, anything more disgraceful to ourselves. And yet, perhaps, no system of cultivating the soil gives a better return to the producer or consumer from the land occupied.

CHAPTER V.

CHARACTERS OF PLANTS.

IN arranging scenery the Characters of Plants must be kept true, else confusion will be the result. In Plant life there is a vast diversity, with form and colour corresponding. The structure of organs is evergreen or deciduous—a circumstance that must affect their arrangement, as well as their arrangement according to vegetable growths. One must study the feeling produced by their forms and colours, as well as the results of their combination in respect of outlines, or the massing of leaf, or fruit, or flower, at different periods of the year. Plants not only display various effects during the course of the season, but even during the lapse of years. They vary, for example, in their youth, their perfect growth, and their decline. When we are well aware of the features attendant on different periods of Plant life, we discriminate between the effects at all stages of development and decay, and can the better avail ourselves of the various beauties and perfections of vegetable life.

Even at their full development, trees are often found to vary in dimensions, and therefore it is that each plant must be studied by and in itself, conveying thus a vast mass of information. Surely it is a thing of great moment that a name should impart something of the character of species, as is the case with the *Populus fastigiata*, or columnar Poplar, reminding us of their beauty, and, if it might be, their economic uses as well. Books of reference and specimens are available to any extent in a capital, though such privileges rarely exist in the provinces. Something, surely, might be done by the Royal Horticultural, and other societies, to remedy this deficiency, and otherwise to promote the knowledge and rectify the terminology of plants.

In respect of the arrangement of scenery, it will be desirable to determine by observation the results produced by foreground and distance. To do this effectively, it will be needful to place the eye alternately close at hand and remote. We shall thus obtain a general

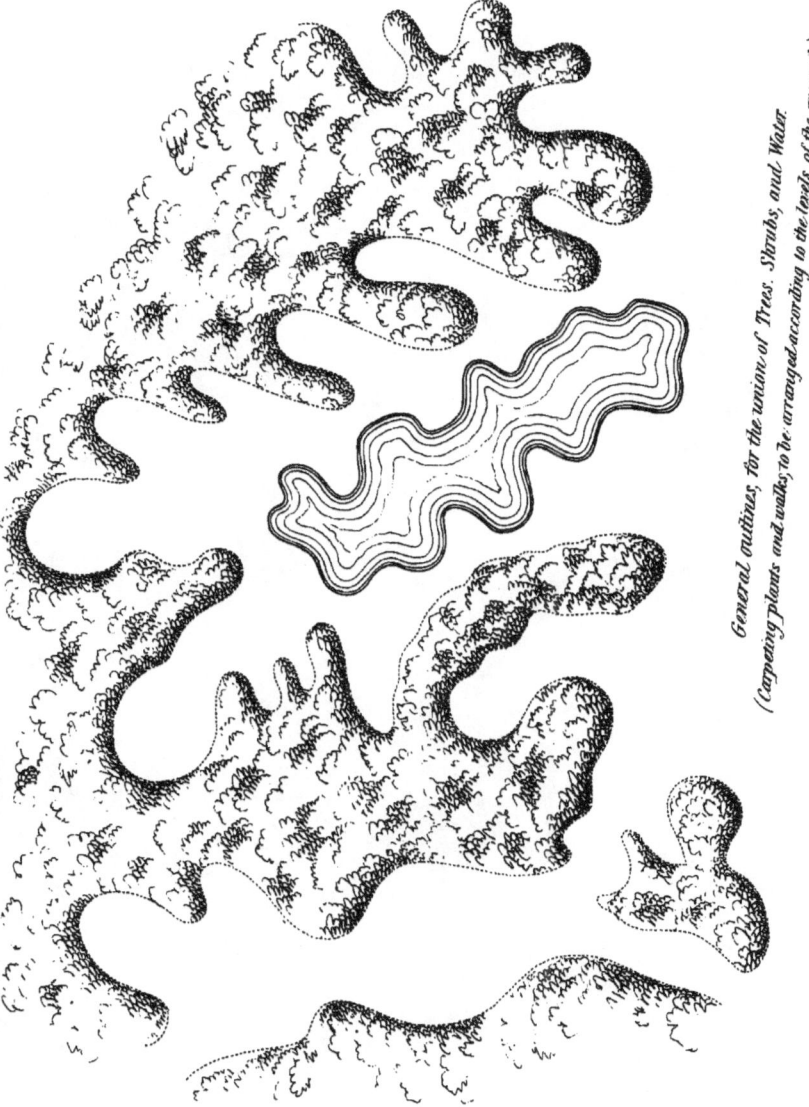

Plate 6

General outlines, for the union of Trees, Shrubs, and Water. (Creeping plants and walks, to be arranged according to the levels of the ground.)

knowledge of outline and effect, of the leafage and form of plants, both as foreground and distant objects, so that, look which way we will, we shall be able to determine the true effect from foot to sky.

Form is undoubtedly the basis of arrangement, but colour gives life to form. Colour may sometimes have prominence for its own sake, but still it should embellish and set off form. Lights and shades are also attendants on colour, and must have due consideration. Colour is as the magic touchstone of scenery, mysteriously enhancing its effects. No language, indeed, will prove adequate to set forth its wondrous influence. All scenery demands a careful selection of materials founded on the principles of form, aiding the landscape wherever it may be found deficient. The lines of vegetation vary, imparting suitable features in accordance with the period of the year. These features may be summed under the nine following heads :— Outline, massing, young leafage, perfect leafage, fall of leaf, flower, fruit, stem, dimensions.

In many trees all these characteristics are more or less specially developed, as, for example, in the genera *Æsculus* and *Salix*. A catalogue of Plants to enumerate the above effects in detail would be most useful as a reference in all arrangements of arboreal vegetable growths, also for increasing the general knowledge of character.

Thus the effects peculiar to each growth should be the subject of careful study ; and, in order to acquire a complete knowledge of these, we should need to prosecute our researches in various localities. Much that would have been of value has been lost through a system of regarding only one effect of a plant as worthy of attention, instead of turning to account every effect, at all periods of the year.

Among the varying parts of Plants, we shall generally be able to select those that will aid us in our efforts to produce harmonious results. The delicate details of leafage come within easy range of vision, while masses of foliage and general outlines of trees can be only seen from afar off. Particulars concerning the various forms of leaves, as stated in many books, will be found extremely useful in making arrangements to be seen close at hand, and also at a distance. Leafage, properly considered, will often be a great assistance towards gaining a knowledge of the characters of vegetation. Those intermediate growths, called Shrubs, should be arranged, firstly, according to their masses, and, secondly, in accordance with their outlines. Trees, on the other hand, should be arranged, in the first place, according to outline, and, in the second, according to their masses. Grounds planted with Rhododendrons have a very rich character. The effect of their undulations and foliage massing and outlines, loaded with brilliant flowers, may be much enhanced by borrowing hues of silver and gold from other plants, more especially at the season when Rhododendron flowers are scarce. Their masses of rounded foliage gain much by being contrasted with growths of columnar and horizontal form.

As regards Flower Gardens, we might say that our chief aim is to produce a beautiful, brilliant effect, at least at some one period of the year. Thus the brilliant effect of the Flower Garden, or the rich effect of the Rhododendron, should not be destroyed, but developed into their natural beauty.

One sometimes sees the delicate beauty of a Rosetum very much impaired by planting near it flowers of vivid colouring, such as Scarlet Pelargoniums, with the mistaken view of enhancing the effect. Such errors must, if possible, be avoided in every case, for it is the individual aspect that has the greatest charm for us. If we desire to preserve the true character of a scene, our arrangements must always be harmonious. Indeed, the natural growth of plants should, as I have before said, be the subject of our most earnest study. These in our Nurseries are frequently so treated, as, for example, when cut for propagation, that they cease to manifest their true character; the plant very often displaying a compact, close growth by no means proper to it. Hollies might often be cited as an instance of this, varieties that, in a natural state, show fine, undulating masses of foliage, evincing quite a different appearance in the Nursery grounds.

Scenery is composed of a vast aggregate of details, each distinct and each true to its individual character. A wide scope, however, yet remains for progress as regards our Horticultural arrangements.

So many vegetable forms have at different times been introduced from abroad that very often plants belonging to the same genus display very various aspects. The Oaks *(Quercus)*, the Ivies *(Hedera)*, and other genera are examples of this. Yet not seldom arrangers act as though but one kind of Ivy were available, whereas in reality we possess many varieties, some beautiful as miniature shrubs, others clinging so firmly to masonry that one might suppose they formed a portion of the solid stone, while the glossy shining leaves display an infinite diversity of form. The same remarks hold good with respect to Hollies and Rhododendrons. Too frequently, however, in our arrangements, the various growths are all mixed together, giving a confusion of form and colour to the mind. Confusion is not beauty: therefore plants require to be arranged together which have some true comparison to each other. Natural scenery is everywhere replete in loveliness, but all are not equally alive to it. We can but receive that which we bring, and it is only to those whose hearts and minds are open, that Nature displays her secrets and her beauties.

We need never seek to compass successful results by mere change. The requirements of the ground should be studied, and the latter planted in accordance with them. Each year will then be found to bring forth new beauties, or disclose fresh effects, which shall, in fine, become sources of unceasing pleasure. How often do we see the green sward, when laid out, despoiled of all its natural undulations, made level and straight. The beautiful carpet spread for man's delight and service, is made to look as unlike Nature's handiwork as possible. Again, we may see a mixed border dotted with about two dozen forms of the same species, instead of each variety being grouped together, covering an allotted space of ground. Affecting change for the sake of change is as great an error as that of acting always according to rule and measure.

It is most requisite that our landscapes should manifest character. This result will greatly depend on the arrangement and choice displayed in our subjects. They will also borrow much from the resemblance of leafage, which will often lead onwards to the characteristics of form, and even where the massing and outlines of trees compose the subject to be arranged, the leafage will assist to judge the true character of these subjects. Not always will the leafage be the guide, but it will be the chief characteristic of a certain form of vegetation, forming a base to the study of effects, as in the carpeting plants *Stachys lanata*, *Salvia argentea*, &c. Some of the genera, such as *Cistus*, *Mimulus*, *Phlomis*, &c., take the form of woollyness; others, as the *Digitalis*, *Hesperis*, *Mentha*, *Symphytum*, *Verbascum*, and others, all take a stronger impression of being woolly or hairy. See the varieties of minute leaves among the beautiful *Helianthemum*, *Lithospermum prostratum*,

H

Polygonum vaccinifolium, Cerastiums of various sorts, and *Arenaria balearica*. Although *Pentstemons* are not quite like the curious flowers of the *Antirrhinum*, still I always think they are not unsuitably placed together. The curious flowers of *Monarda* and *Linaria* are, I think, suited as associates to the *Antirrhinums*, as curious effects. The leaves of the *Primula, Alyssum, Gentiana acaulis, Campanula*, and *Lobelia fulgens* have some characters in common. Each genera has many species suitable to be placed together, particularly as their flowers can easily be grown to succeed each other. The great variety of such plants as *Saxifraga Sedum* are enough to vary the colour and form of the ground, to a great extent, where required. Ivies are peculiarly valuable for the ground line of effects. Many of these low growing plants possess characteristics suitable for a profusion of scenes, which should be governed in accordance with the general character of the scenery to be arranged.

Unlimited harmonious effects may be made amongst the following genera of plants—*Hepatica, Erodium, Hedera, Sanguinaria, Sibthorpia, Heracleum, Gunnera, Malva, Aconitum, Delphinium, Cannabis, Astrantia, Trollius, Geranium, Lupinus*. The celebrated *Acanthus* forms may be assisted in their effects by such plants as *Scabiosa, Centaurea, Dipsacus, Papaver, Francoa, Lychnis, Lythrum, Scrophularia, Mornia, Polemonium*, and *Bocconia cordata*. The Anemones might fringe many forms of vegetation, and be particularly suited for making grounds or margins to such plants as the fine old Columbines, *(Aquilegia)* Lupines, and the Adiantum—like *Thalictrum* and *Epimedium*. How often is a particular effect of plant form destroyed, through being overpowered by the mixtures adjacent thereto having no respect for any principle. Thus does one feature destroy the other, whereas when a principle is acknowledged in each effect, every plant may show harmony in serving the principle, or in being the principle itself of the scene, exhibiting its special beauty in due time. Sometimes a few Sedums and Saxifrages are seen placed together without suitable surroundings, and the minute leafage or fine foliage of plants is rarely ever shewn as the principle of a scene, and exhibited by contrast and strength. Where do we find exhibited the fineness of foliage possessed by many plants, except in the masses of the native species of *Erica*, on the mountains?

Plate 7

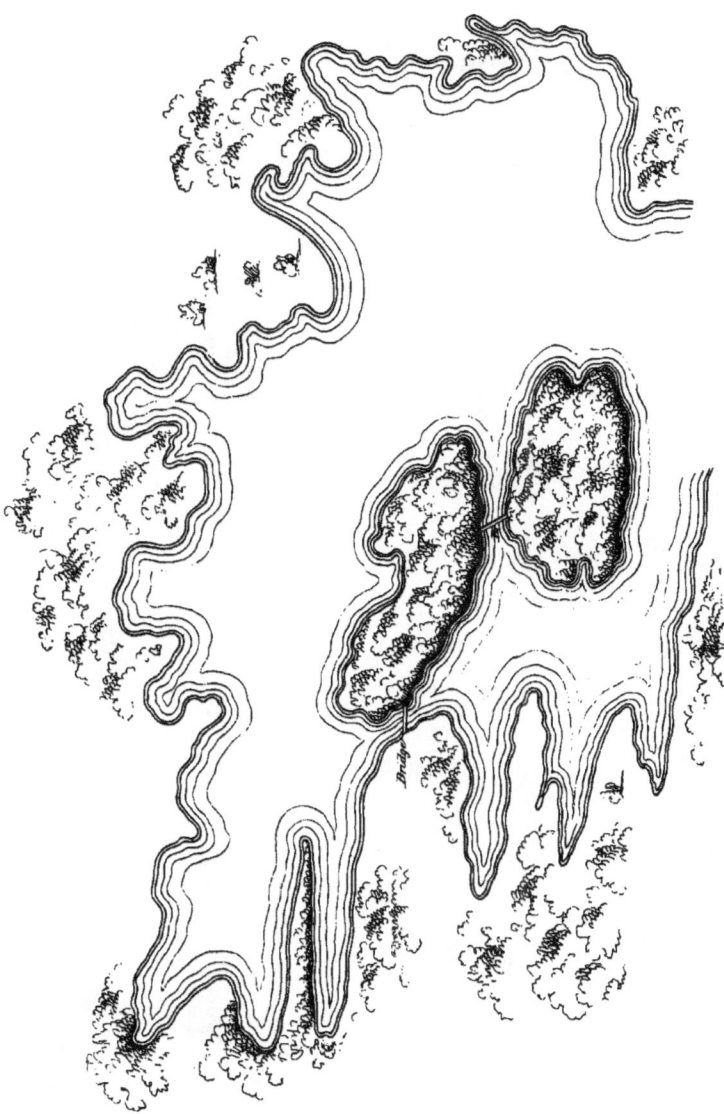

Outlines of water for a lawn, suitable to receive the benefit of vegetation.

The delicate foliaged plants would make delicate effects by being placed in comparison with other plants of a similar character and contrast, so as to bring out the effects and not destroy them, as *Arenaria balearica, Pæonia tenuifolia*, and many species of the genera *Achillea, Asperula, Asphodelus, Astragulus, Euphorbia, Pyrethrum, Seseli*, &c. All these, and various other plants, have delicate forms which vary much from each other, and yet have a sufficient general resemblance to be arranged into various features in the same character, when a principle is taken as the guiding point in choosing the material required for the character of the scene to be decorated.

One of the horrors of garden arrangement is the feeling displayed in the want of change. Plants cruelly cut into dots, and tied into bundles, were justly the ruin of the border system; and unless a more beautiful way is taken to exhibit their effects, their ruin will soon recommence. Should a suitable natural system be adopted, they will increase in favour from year to year, for the lapse of time will add to them beauty upon beauty. The first year many species keep small, and it requires time for numbers of them to so cover the ground that they may exhibit their effects. This wretched and fanciful system of changing when there is nothing to change, is perfectly demoralizing. It is easy to observe a mixed border containing, on the average, about two dozen dots of each species; and if you ask why they are not grouped together, covering their share of the ground in two or three places, instead of two dozen you will often receive a look of contempt for not discovering the perfection of this miserable arrangement of plants, which, in the hands of men who do know something of good taste, are only made passable. The rule and the square have been held before gardeners too much at this point of their profession.

CHARACTERS OF SHRUBS.

The vegetable growths which we term Shrubs generally attract much attention by means of leaves, or flowers, or fruit, or massing, or outlines, displaying various effects at different seasons. As far as I have been able to learn, the massing and general outlines of Shrubs have not received the attention they deserve. Shrubs display beautiful outlines in their own natural growth.

The small details of plant life have received much thought from horticulturists; but the massing and general outlines of their undulations have not received the attention in arrangement that their effects merit, particularly in the larger forms of vegetation, which have been almost ignored, and are all but neglected. Although these two effects of vegetation—outlines and masses—produce an impression, more or less, on every person, for you cannot pass a Shrub or Tree, even buried in thought, without receiving an invisible influence, communicated by their masses and outlines, yet the details must have one's particular attention before one can see them. But the subjects that surround you, guide your path, and meet every view of your eyes, shedding an influence over your life such as every person is not aware of; therefore the general outlines and massing of vegetation should be carefully adjusted, and on these two features of character I will venture to give a few remarks in the following pages.

Every feature of plant life should be undoubtedly studied, and its beauties exhibited. I do not say that the details have received too much thought, but I do believe the massing and outlines have received too little. When you are in proximity to a Shrub, you see the beauties of its leaves; retire to a distance, and you will see the beauty of its masses of foliage; retire still further, and you will see the beauty of its general outlines. If every line of sight receives the proper care belonging to the character of its vegetation, it will all be beautiful from every site; thus, from your feet as far as the eye can see, each distance has its own effect. Any position should be able to exhibit both foreground, mid-distance, and remote distance, all in good arrangement, for quite near to you the details are most conspicuous; in the mid-distance you see those details forming into masses, and in the distance you see the masses forming the general order of their outlines. Thus small subjects are to be arranged in masses for mid-distances, and masses formed into general outlines for the distance, or general effect. These are points very much neglected in the present arrangements of the beautifiers of land, and which require much study before any success can be gained by their arrangement. The completion of the lines of sight, of whatever character arranged, is so neglected that I have ventured to repeat myself above intentionally.

Plant life possesses so many characteristics that the mind requires to be always open to receive conviction of their many effects; not so much to compare one plant to be better than another, which is false comparison, as to compare plants together to increase each other's beauty, which is true comparison, and to find the proper place for the same by endeavouring to develop the beauties of each subject.

Plants in our grounds are often more or less packed together, exhibiting a very unnatural aspect, their true character being quite ignored. The common Holly is seldom tended so as to develop all its beauty. It will, when properly cared for, be covered with brilliant scarlet berries. It grows upwards of twenty feet in height, giving deep undulations of fine romantic forms, being rich in lights and shades, and it is always effective, from carpeting the ground as a shrub, until it develops its beauty as a tree.

In the *Ilex* there are indeed so many varieties of growth, as regards form and colour, that these would almost prove sufficient in themselves to diversify a landscape in a most pleasing, romantic manner, which would produce charming effects, that would gain admiration for many years without further labour, when once properly established. *Picea Pinsapo* shows the same quaint character of shades, I fancy, as the common Holly.

The *Cerasus Laurocerasus*, generally known as the common Laurel, is frequently made use of near buildings, being well adapted for forming good banks of evergreen by pruning into suitable forms, though in this way the beauty of the plant is not developed, as it becomes a part of the building effects. This variety of Laurel, however, does not suit well for covering ground; it has, so to speak, a wild character of growth, stretching out its arms (branches) in all directions. It is, on the other hand, very serviceable for veiling distant elevations of shrubbery, particularly in wild effects. There are, however, various forms of Laurel, all possessing characters which may often be turned to valuable account.

The genus *Taxus* also, when contrasted with other forms of vegetation, or when used in comparison, produces excellent effects on landscapes. It possesses many features within itself, particularly valuable for mellowing distant lights and shades. All this suggests very important points in land decoration. The *Taxus* also possesses many distinctive varieties of outline, which, with its dark colouring and minute leafage, will be found very conducive to many effects, its golden forms producing great richness. The *Taxus baccata* (common Yew) is found to thrive where hardly any other evergreen will flourish, such as upon roots of trees, even those of the Elm and Beech, and under these circumstances, instead of striking out and yielding foliage aloft, will very often suffice to carpet the ground for many years. In beds of common English Yew, which have been raised from seed, a great variety of forms will sometimes exist, some taking the vertical, others the horizontal form of development. I saw a variety of the *Taxus baccata Daviesii* which had assumed a perfectly pyramidal aspect, which Mr. Davis, of Hillsborough, stated had not been done with the knife. Many and varied are the forms named in the catalogues of nurserymen. Plants of the *Taxus* display their character long before they become too large to remove. They possess, indeed, masses of fibrous roots, which permits them to be removed even after they attain to a large growth. The infinite variety and density of foliage, particularly in the case of the Irish Yew, when turned to proper account, produce results at once suggestive of admiration and awe, calculated to endure for ages.

The common Yew is suitable for dark shades necessary for scenery, as underneath trees, hollow grounds, &c., and the deep shades in developing the outlines of scenery, being one of the very best plants we possess for this purpose, as well as assisting the ground lines to develop other forms and colours of vegetation. The Yew imparts a character or feeling of patience ; as, for example, a scene of the Irish Yew, *Taxus baccata fastigiata*, gives the "noble passion of awe" with a wonderful depth of feeling.

Rhododendrons.—Of all the various plants which we possess, there are none, so far as I know, that have not an individual beauty of their own. Many of our Shrubs are employed to carpet the ground, and, as it were, to break the monotony of the view. Some, however, which are used for this purpose, Holly and Laurel for instance, are quite unsuitable. No growths, perhaps, are better calculated to yield successful results in this respect than the many varieties of *Rhododendrons*. Their varieties preserve a complete and natural outline close to the ground, without the aid of cutting and trimming—a matter of very great importance as regards Shrubs that are required to break the ground-line permanently, and serve as connecting lines

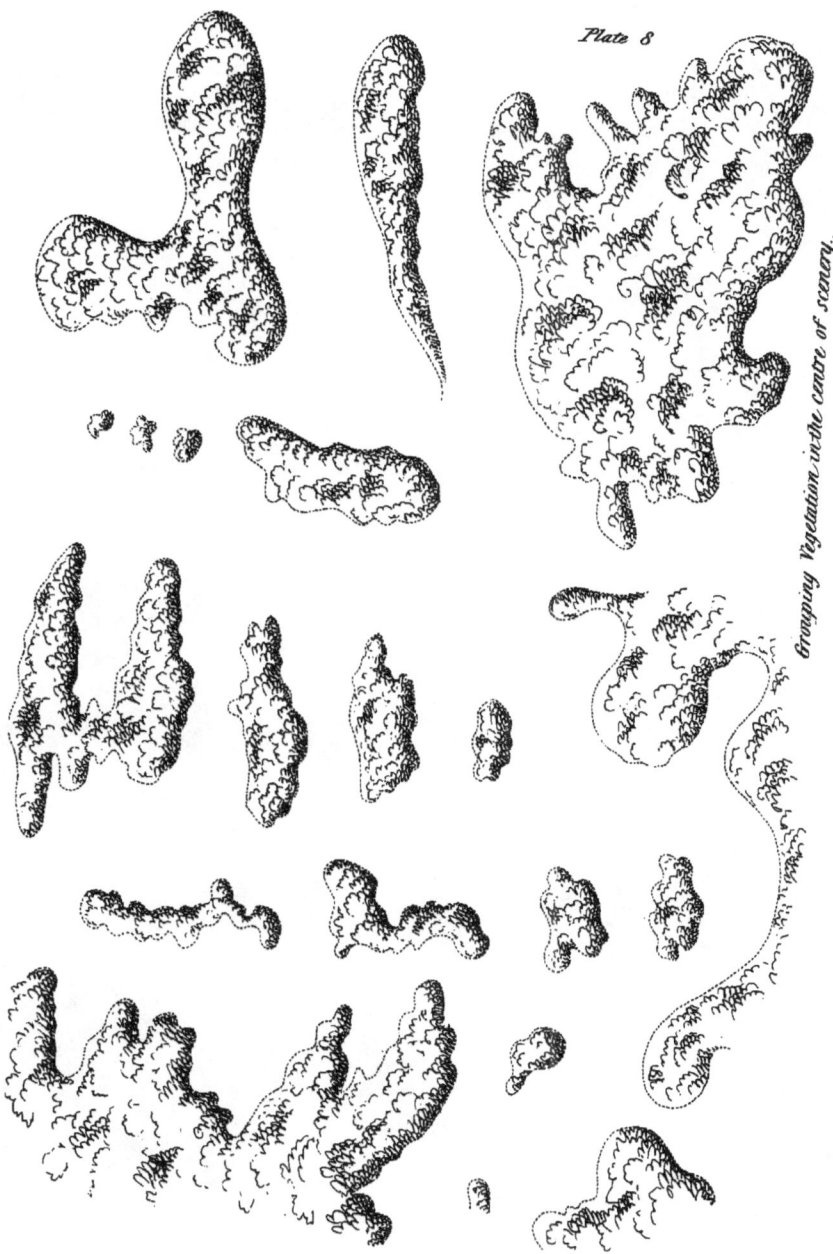

Plate 8

Grouping Vegetation in the centre of scenery.

between carpeting plants and the loftier forms of vegetation. The common *Rhododendron ponticum* is an evergreen Shrub possessing great endurance ; it is both rounding in its mass and outline, and rich in the effects of its undulations. The young leafage in spring is delicately erect, and charming to look at, while the leafage when more matured is arranged in graceful whorls. The beautifully subdued tints and rounding general outlines of the foliage furnish, indeed, in many cases, a most desirable basis for effects of large growths of vegetation. The blossoms greatly enhance the aspect of ornamental grounds, for they (together with other Shrubs) come at a period when the dwarf spring flowers are nearly gone, while those of summer are not yet developed. Some plant in the middle line of sight should be more or less general to give union. The *Rhododendron* is a very suitable plant for this purpose, instead of such plants as naturally are without bottom foliage enough to break the ground line, like the common Laurel, which is often used all over the ground, though it is highly inexpedient to bring it into too general use for backgrounds, hollows, and the like, for in this way it often fails to develop the effects proper to these positions, while at the same time it occupies the ground that more suitable growths would fitly embellish. In using Rhododendrons as a union, a single plant will in many places continue this effect in some places, so that they interfere not with the principal character. The Rhododendron is beautiful when employed to realise a leading effect in scenery, particularly when surrounded by vegetation of a darker shade than its own, such, for example, as is witnessed in many species of the Fir tribe. These again ought to be contrasted with lighter hues and more silvery colours on the heights. The flowers of the Rhododendron range from the most brilliant to the most delicate hues. The latter, however, should not be placed in too great proximity to strong tints, while white, again, ought to have a little prominence above other shades. Purple, with its many gradations, is very suitable for the decoration of the low-lying ground of a Rhododendron scene. Gold, as already stated, we must borrow from other growths. Ruskin, I think, says somewhere that the Rhododendron is the most beautiful of all our Shrubs, and it would be difficult indeed to over-estimate the effects it is capable of yielding. The flowers shine with a vivid loveliness, but seldom produced in our climate by any other plant.

The Rhododendron is, in truth, amongst Shrubs, the Queen of Harmony. Hooker relates how he once beheld on one of the slopes of the Sikkim Himalaya a space of ten thousand acres covered with this plant in full flower. Anything more glorious, he states, it would be impossible to imagine or describe. Although we cannot grow out-doors many of the Indian varieties, still we have varieties enough of the Rhododendron to produce scenes of magnificent richness.

There are numerous Shrubs possessing important characters, as, for example, in the following genera:—*Berberis, Buxus, Arbutus, Cystisus* (Broom), *Ceanothus, Cistus, Cotoneaster, Daphne, Colletia, Elæagnus, Euonymus, Gaultheria, Garrya, Ivies, Kalmia, Jasminum, Magnolia, Mahonia, Phillyrea, Pittosporum, Rhamnus, Yucca,* and many others. Among these will be found many species suitable for our purposes, always bearing in mind the character of the ground. The deciduous Shrubs, again, are of great value on account of the effects produced by their leafage, flowers, and general outline. The *Althæa frutex* in many cases yields a profusion of flowers. The *Buddlea globosa* is often very effective; the leaves of this plant are soft in character, while the flowers, which resemble small golden balls, give the plant a singular appearance. The following genera possess many varieties which will be found most useful for decorative purposes:— *Cratægus, Cydonia, Deutzia, Sambucus, Syringa, Philadelphus, Ribes, Spiræa, Rhus,* and *Weigela*. Much of the art of arranging vegetation consists in placing the character of the plants planted into harmony suitable to the scene intended to beautify.

CHARACTERS OF TREES.

In the arrangement of these most important members of the vegetable kingdom, it is absolutely incumbent on us to consider well the characters of each. Too often, indeed, do we see plants misplaced producing results the reverse of those that satisfy, and frequently the mischief done is great.

Trees and other forms of plants might be broadly divided into evergreen and deciduous. In trees, the Fir tribe, in many instances, displays exceeding grandeur and nobleness. The effects, in truth, of this tribe individually vie with each other in feelings of nobleness, life, and majesty. The deciduous trees, when ascending to their noblest forms, seem never quite to forget their grace, for they always present more or less, a light, airy effect to the mind. In these two great divisions of vegetation it may be seen how very suitable Nature is to satisfy the feelings of mankind ; for whether it be a strong, intermediate, or delicate effect, each can be supplied in many characters of vegetation. Thus we have material for feeding the mind from light, easy, graceful feelings to grand nobility of character. In this respect, Trees—evergreen and deciduous—do much to satisfy the lines of sight, providing for the eye the necessary feelings for enjoyment, and the arrangement made in their outlines and massing produces the varied effects of mass and infinity to the human mind.

As already said, the chief attention of horticulturists has been devoted to the minuter structure of plants. Their effects at various elevations and distances have been much ignored, if we except that department of Botanical Geography which treats of the distribution of plants in climatological zones of elevation or latitude, and which corresponds somewhat to the relation of plants to landscape effects. One of the results of this has been the slow progress which Horticulture has made in beautifying the earth. But this premised, the study of detail is quite needful to determine the true character of the different forms of vegetation. Persons of sufficient grasp of mind will always be able to lay hold of general principles without allowing themselves to be too much carried away by one beauty to the injury of all others.

Men with practice acquire a sort of instinct in arrangement for which it is not always easy to give reasons. Novelty may excite and be pleasing from its newness, but it cannot satisfy—which I venture to say is necessary to any object for beauty. After a little time, novelty itself, with whatever pomp of circumstance, will tire. Decorated land should increase in pleasure as it becomes better known. Survey the nearest forest tree, and watch its changes day by day ; presently a profound liking will spring up for it, and a disgust for those artificial arrangements of cut forms, which wealth, not (good) taste, has served to create, and a more correct feeling as nearly banished them from this country. Nature, indeed, is never alike on every side. On each rising undulation of land there are different forms ; while on the vegetation itself, there is lavished a world of diversity in clearness of beauty, which the hand of man must follow in its principles. Look

I

as often as you will, and still new beauties unfold themselves, varying according to the character of the individual who surveys them; but not to any greater extent—for light is light, blackness is blackness, &c., to all who can see.

In the arrangement of trees, the one important thing is to compass combinations which shall prove beautiful. Various results will ensue, according to the distances from which they are surveyed. We shall have to consider the character of our foreground leafage (which is already minutely done in botanical works), as well as that which is more remote. I will venture to affirm that the character of trees must be individually studied, before we shall be fully able to appreciate their outlines and effects. It will be impossible, otherwise, to succeed in evoking in the human mind the feelings which it is our necessary object to produce for proper arrangement.

The *Outlines* and *Massing* of vegetation contain infinite varieties of unarranged effects. The Upright Poplar, the Cedar of Lebanon, and Round-topped Trees, seem to embody all the feeling some arrangers can think of; thus they show that they know little, either of the wants of mankind or the powers of vegetation. I will endeavour, therefore, to state a few features chiefly belonging to these two.

TABULAR TREES.

The evergreen forms of these with horizontal branches, possess a superiority over the deciduous. The Cedar of Lebanon, *Cedrus Libani*, is not only well known, but generally, greatly admired, yet still it is not much planted. Nothing, perhaps, can well surpass its majestic dignity. I know nothing to approach its effect in its own character when properly introduced. It evinces the greatest power of imparting unity to scenery, as well as of enhancing works of art themselves, such as terraces, the extensive façades of buildings, and the like. In other respects, however, small villas are more the accessories of scenery than the essentials. Indeed, wherever the soil is suitable, the *Cedrus Libani* should always find a place. One of the first things which, as a child, I can remember, was a tree of this species. *Cedrus Atlantica* is sometimes wrongly used instead of *Cedrus Libani*, as its foliage is light enough to give light to the high ground of a Cedar vale, when compared with the rich dark masses of the Cedar of Lebanon.

PLATE 11

Juniperus excelsa var.

Pinus sylvestris

Cratægus Crusgalli pyracanthifolia
(Summer effect)

Cratægus Crusgalli pyracanthifolia
(Winter effect)

Some individuals of the common Yew, *Taxus baccata*, occasionally assume the Tabular form, and can thus, when their character is matured, be turned to excellent account. This is also the case with some deciduous trees, as, for example—the *Cratægus crusgalli pyracanthifolia*, which, by its flowers in spring and foliage in summer, as well as by its grey and silvery bark in winter, realises very important effects. It is very suitable to small buildings, as a part of the surrounding scenery, and, though Loudon pointedly adverted to it with encomium some years ago, it is not nearly so often planted as it undoubtedly deserves to be. (See PLATE 11, page 67.) The light-coloured fern-leaved Beech, *Fagus heterophylla*, forms a flat top, and is excellent for gardens and small lawns, yielding shade without any undue pretentiousness.

PYRAMIDAL OUTLINES, VERTICAL LEADERS, AND HORIZONTAL BRANCHES.

Picea.—The genus *Picea* contains growths of various forms. The chief distinguishing feature of this group of Firs, is their erect pyramidal outline, towering into the air by a straight central leading stem like a line of life; the branches of foliage, in general, display a beautiful character of symmetry, arranged in horizontal masses. Many of these plants are of the very greatest service in decoration, but it is a pity to employ them, as is sometimes done, merely to line our walks. Some species of *Picea* reach a height of 200 feet, as, for example—the *Picea amabilis*, *Picea nobilis*, *Picea grandis*, and *Picea lasiocarpa*, the latter even, it is said, attaining in North California, an elevation of 280 feet. Alternating as the shades of these trees do, from the darkest hues to ones of silvery lightness, the effects imparted by them to our scenery are often strikingly lovely in the extreme. They are scarcely well adapted, however, for close proximity to buildings, their forms presenting too much life appearance contrasted with the dead walls and square outlines of houses. Were a mansion, indeed, constructed with regard to effect, presenting to view a number of pointed embellishments and the like, then it is most probable that many of our *Picea* might be employed with great advantage, but their airy aspect will not be found to suit with unvarying lines of brick or stone. For avenues, the so-termed umbrageous trees will be more desirable than Firs. The object of an avenue is generally to conduct visitors to a mansion, an object which should not, therefore, be lost sight of. The beauty of this type of Fir trees, mostly continues for very many years, when sufficient space is allowed for their development; whether as foreground, single specimens, or as groups. In their early stages they clothe the very ground, then rising, their massive branches seem as though binding earth and sky together. The Chestnut avenue in Bushy Park is one of the grandest things anywhere to be seen, and may be truly said to have yielded solace and satisfaction to millions. These Firs, however, with their hundreds of branches, taking the most opposite directions, filling the eye from ground to summit, render them very suitable as individual trees, each complete in itself, and yet forming a portion of some other and more general effect, such as promontories, and grouping therefrom.

The Fir tribe is often badly used, and their character destroyed by injudicious handling, such as planting them in confused masses to the ruin of each other. It is impossible for trees, under such circumstances, to be perfectly mature and give their character to our feelings. It is, in fact, contrary to Nature. A good tree, indeed, when visible, gains respect and protection from all; but when huddled together, trees confuse the eye, and express no character but confusion. No good house can be constructed with unsuitable materials, and it is just as difficult to fix a landscape when it has no character with which to develop the land beauty, or when the characters are unfitted to each other in the succession of effects. As these pages are merely intended to set forth principles, details are only given to endeavour to make the meaning plain.

ROUND-HEADED TREES.

Of these, so-termed, there are many varieties, which suit well amid forest and wooded scenery generally. They do not, however, in every case display the semi-circular curves of outlines which, as some would seem to have us believe, prove their only mode of growth. Yet how rarely do we observe successful effects of trees blending with each other for want of attention being given to the characters of each, such as we witness sometimes even in Nature's wild woodland scenery. The old English Oak *(Quercus pedunculata)* is properly entitled to the first place in virtue of its picturesque beauty, and of which Gilpin has so truly said, "It adds dignity to a ruined tower." From early associations we have come to look upon it as a bulwark of the country. It takes rather angular forms in its round general outlines, and in the massing of foliage innumerable angularities are shewn, varying greatly, as can be seen in a wood of this timber. Some come into leaf with a most beautiful golden leafage, while others are of a greener colour. They also vary in time, from a week to a fortnight, in putting forth their leaves. This difficulty can be corrected in the early stages of their growth, either in the reserve ground or even in the decorated land. The English Oak is well suited for wild romantic scenery; thus Wordsworth speaks of it—

"An oak,
Hardy and grand, a weather-beaten oak,
Fresh in the strength and majesty of age,
And one whose roots by noontide dews were damped,
And on whose forehead inaccessible
The raven lodged in safety."

Our Evergreen Trees generally display spiral heads instead of the rounded tops that characterise deciduous ones. The *Quercus Ilex* is the finest, or among the finest of the Evergreens which we possess, and it is pleasing to observe that more interest is yearly taken in its behalf in ornamental planting. It is better adapted for the sea coast than most others, and I have even seen it reach an elevation of fifty feet in such a situation. During the severe winter of 1870-71 a number of them became deciduous, and yet afforded a good display of leaves the following summer; but as our winters are rarely so cold we need be under no apprehension that they should become deciduous. These plants vary much in their outlines and masses. Evergreen Oaks are not all round-headed. *Pinus Pinea* also makes a good small roundish headed evergreen tree.

The *Ulmus campestris*, or English Elm, will load itself with branches for many years, just above the browsing height of cattle. Its lower limbs and broad massive sides harmonise advantageously with its large round head; the branches would almost seem conscious of their importance, and delight in an exuberance of foliage for a long succession of seasons. It masses its foliage in round forms, in dense shades and lights, the shades often taking triangular forms. Its lower branches are nearly horizontal from the main stem, but, as they near the top, each takes a more upright form until they cluster round the top of the tree like a goblet.

The *Ulmus montana*, or Scotch Elm, is very different in its character. Its head assumes a much more round umbrageous character, while its masses being large and few, it is enabled to yield a most refreshing deep shade.

Acer.—The Maple varies much in effect according to the species. It has become a very favourite plant on lawns. It assumes a very agreeable irregularity of outline, in graceful curves arranging its masses of foliage in large oval forms, often assuming a nearly horizontal outline when its characters are developed. This tree has been a universal favourite with mankind in many ages. According to Theocritus, the virgins of Sparta used to assemble around some Plane Tree and sing. The foliage of the *Acer Pseudo-Platanus* is productive of deep lights and shades, engendering the richest effects in suitable scenery.

The *Tilia europæa* scarcely shows any branches amid its formal pyramidal mass, as they are covered with a most becoming garment of light green foliage, the leaves seeming to arrange themselves in laces about the tree. The perfume of the flowers of the Lime is grateful to many.

The *Castanea vesca*, or Sweet Chestnut, is one of the stateliest of trees. It is a good summer tree, particularly when covered with its beautiful leafage, and clusters of fair tinted flowers. Its masses give beautiful deep light and shade and bold undulations in their outlines. Its rounded top being small, when compared with that of other trees, is apt to arrange itself into a pyramidal form, with large masses at the bottom, which become less towards the top. This tree possesses much of the picturesque effects of the Oak in its old age, but is less rugged in character.

Salix Russelliana is one of the most complete round-headed trees in its outlines, possessing a most powerful rugged stem. It gives much shade on the ground, and it has a wild aristocratic effect among other trees.

Betula Alba is one of those trees which give picturesque beauty, being romantic in its massing and outlines. It is a most useful tree for winter effects from its white bark shining amid its dark branchlets, and, although romantic, its character is not wild, thereby enabling it to assist many effects in scenery. Thus Wordsworth—

> "In the dry crannies of the pendant rocks,
> Light birch aloft upon the horizons edge,
> A veil of glory for the ascending moon."

Fagus Sylvatica, or common Beech, if judged in the perfect leafage of July, or in the bare branches of winter, will not convey at those periods that satisfaction in its beauty which it will give at others. In spring, for instance, its wild sharp outlines and angular massing of foliage begin to show themselves. The deep shades in the hollows of its massing, the high lights on the prominences, are all soon clothed in leafage of most delicate formation, rising in waves above waves of surpassing beauty. Its colour, so clear, golden, and shining, gleaming forth in innocence, unrivalled in sylvan majesty, it may be crowned Spring's Virgin Queen. The autumn tints of the Beech are often very good in rich colours. In old age, the lower branches of the trees often droop gracefully.

Populus.—Most of the varieties of the Poplar are very ornamental, more especially in early spring. The *Populus nigra* is frequently seen towering above other trees, producing very striking effects. Some fine specimens of this plant possess occasionally as many as four or five leading stems, forming acute outlines. The foliage, which in spring is singularly light and graceful, possesses hues which cause it to contrast favourably with most other leafage, and their early growths can be discerned for miles. The masses are long and regular in form, with a direct upward tendency. The leafage is particularly light in appearance in this and other Poplars, which in the least breeze appear as if flying about the branches like humming birds. The rapid growth of this tree is a circumstance generally well known, and one which renders it very serviceable in cases where we wish to produce sudden effects, or where it is found desirable to shelter other plants. There are numerous Poplars, some of which possess very distinct characters, as the stately Lombardy Poplar, the Sighing Poplar or Aspen, *Populus tremula*, and the *Populus argentea*, &c., each possessing its own quality as respects the duration of the timber. I may quote here the old distich said to be found inscribed on a plank of the Poplar tree :—

> "Though heart of oak be e'er as stout,
> Keep me dry, and I'll see him out."

Acacia or *Robinia*.—The foliage of the Acacia or Locust Tree is attractive in the extreme, more especially when it is decked with a profusion of flowers, according to their species, their varying colours, &c., showing more or less of a rustic, romantic character.

Some trees there are, so diminutive in aspect, they might well be termed shrubs. Such trees, however, are often extremely useful, more especially when serving as connecting links between their larger and smaller brethren. They may, for convenience sake, be classed, some as trees, others as shrubs, according to their character and outlines. There are numerous varieties of the so-called Round-headed Trees, which, if you do but look at them, you will find that they have something more than this too general term.

PENDULOUS TREES.

The Pendulous, or, so termed, Weeping Trees, vary greatly in appearance ; still their drooping character is, in many instances, their leading feature, instead of their outlines, as in other trees. Their outlines vary much, both amongst evergreen and deciduous forms, and become suitable for decorating many places by the variety they undoubtedly give in massing and outline, as compared with the Columnar, Round-headed, and Pyramidal forms. Some are capable of realising most imposing results, when these are not neutralised by utter want of judgment. They should always be placed in harmony with the landscape and its surroundings. Instances of the use, or perhaps I ought to say the misuse, of the *Fraxinus excelsior pendula*, or Weeping Ash, and of certain varieties of *Salix*, or Weeping Willow, are often not far to seek, being unsuitably placed in reference to the surroundings, and frequently occupying the point of a promontory where strength of character is wanted. In water scenery strong, effective drooping plants may often be used with the greatest success. There are, indeed, so many varieties that we can always, without too much difficulty, select those with forms of outline and massing which shall suit our decorations. Recesses are well adapted for weeping plants ; still they require plants of a towering outline for assistance, and to serve as a comparison to the drooping outlines, to advance their union to the natural outline, which then may be made to serve as guides or introductions to the scene. Water, again, forms, if I may so term it, the very best basis for the more pendulous varieties, which, in truth, seem as akin to it. Water, which imparts life to all landscapes, yields a fresh charm to these lovely growths. The *Juniperus Sabina*, along with others of like outline, form a pleasing base to weeping trees. These trees also produce very good effects when placed at a little distance from a mansion, or in contiguity to low parapet walls, vases, beds of flowers, and the like. When, however, flower beds are concerned, it will be needful to select plants, the roots of which do not extend along the surface of the ground. Did only space and time permit, I might enlarge yet further concerning this subject.

We shall find, on examination, that the Evergreen Weeping Trees differ in several important respects from the deciduous, and present within themselves many distinct varieties. Some of these trees, members of the Fir tribe for example, are well adapted for small detail promontories. They possess, in general, a columnar or pyramidal character; as for the younger plants, they vary much in respect of outline and massing. Either for foregrounds, or as contributing to distant effects, these trees may be employed to the utmost advantage. The *Cupressus lusitanica* has a somewhat singular pendulous aspect. As for the *Abies excelsa inverta*, it almost startles the spectator with the wild ruggedness of its branches, drooping completely down. The *Thujopsis* varies greatly in the appearance of its columnal outlines. I have seen, at Castle Leslie, the seat of John Leslie, Esq., M.P., a specimen of the *Thujopsis borealis*, which presented a very marked pendulous character, the spray hanging at an acute angle downwards. As for the *Ilex Aquifolium pendula*, or Weeping Holly, it has an almost completely rounded head. We have, indeed, to be particular in selecting spots that harmonise with the outlines of this plant. Places, such as sudden turns in a romantic rockery, however, will often be found to suit it well. The Drooping Yew, *Taxus baccata Dovastoni*, is a good material for enhancing the depths of a weeping group.

The *Cedrus Deodar* forms very beautiful masses of drooping foliage of alternate light and shade. It carpets the very ground with its branches, tinted with silver; then rises in the air with such grace and dignity that it might be justly termed the "Lady of the Garden." This tree, however, often parts with its pendulous character when it attains an elevation above that of ordinary shrubs. It is most valuable in cases in which it proves desirable to realise immediate effects. It will, therefore, be always worth while to keep a number of young plants in stock.

Betula alba pendula.—Even Weeping Trees must be guided by their outlines in arrangement. Pendulous growths that display a certain density and heaviness of outline towards the summit, are well suited for assisting the diversification of hollows in undulations, incident to natural scenery. The Weeping Silver Birch being light at the top, will take a higher position, and is very often a source of considerable effect. And then the roots do not spread much on the surface of the soil, or prove productive of material injury to the various forms of vegetation which carpet the earth. It is well calculated for bowering quiet foot-paths amid spring flowers, besides setting off the lines of beds occupied by level planting. It is, further, occasionally desirable to suffer various climbers to twine around the trees. The common designation of the Pendulous Birch appears to me very suitable—viz., the "Lady of the Forest." The name occurred to me long before I was aware that it had been made use of by Gilpin and others. In studying Nature, the effects which we admire have been often witnessed, and the language that one makes use of is not unfrequently, though unwittingly, repeated. In effect, the Weeping Birch, by its many and changing features, fills every period throughout the year with its beauty, a beauty which it exposes boldly, heedless even of the winter's blast. Its flowing branches wave in pendulous curves with the slightest breath of air. As the spring advances, its profuse leafage shelters its tender branches from the sun's bright rays, and enhances the grace and beauty of everything around.

The Weeping Ash, *Fraxinus excelsior pendula*, is a round-headed tree that stands somewhat in need of assistance from other growths in order to develop its full effects.

The Weeping Lime, *Tilia macrophylla pendula*, has a rather heavy appearance at the summit. The leaves, which are very large, and of a beautiful pale green tint, are so transparent, that one fancies it almost possible to see through them. The *Tilia alba pendula*, though better known, is not so well suited for occupying the high prominences of the foreground as the others above mentioned. It is a plant of strong growth, of rather regular round-headed and dense foliage, which adapts it to more exposed situations in the general low outlines in a glen.

Abies Morinda.—A strange looking plant is the *Abies Morinda*, a drooping conifer, displaying a thick foliage and pyramidal outlines. It presents, indeed, in some cases a quaintness almost approaching to grotesqueness that causes one involuntarily to smile. The genus *Abies* includes many varieties capable of distinct and various expression, as may be witnessed in that choice land of specimens, Dropmore.

The *Abies Canadensis* forms a fine massive tree. It shows an abundance of dense masses of fine airy foliage, and pendulous branches that wave in every breeze that blows. Groups of these plants border the water that flows down the well known vale of Alton Towers, realising very admirable combinations in character, and great power, with its fineness of foliage.

An objection is sometimes made against Weeping Trees, because they are to be seen in cemeteries. But we might as well object to the fair green grass for the same reason. Many other plants, indeed, besides drooping ones, adorn the peaceful tracts which the Germans so touchingly term "God's acres." If this objection is to stand good, all vegetation will have to leave the land, for in cemeteries everything is planted that parties can lay hand on, to all appearances.

Salix.—The Willow, *Salix alba*, towers above many trees, showing its graceful white foliage waving in bold irregular outlines. It flourishes exceedingly along river courses and in other moist situations. It is a beautiful tree to show height, giving elevation to other forms of vegetation. The *Salix babylonica* is particularly deserving of encomium, as a graceful feature in scenery. Its light green foliage responds to the slightest impulse of the breeze, while its bold and irregular outlines enhance the effects of a multitude of other trees. Its good effects near water are well known, but rarely made the best use of.

The Weeping Beech, *Fagus sylvatica pendula*, has a distinct and striking effect, particularly in summer. Its dense green foliage abounds in the greatest variety of alternate lights and shades, while in general appearance it towers up into a pyramid of undulating outlines.

The *Ulmus montana pendula*, or Weeping Elm, displays most irregular rugged outlines. However many you may happen to pass under observation, you are never quite sure that the next individual will not evince outlines almost entirely dissimilar. The foliage droops in pendulous masses from the various branches, as in irregular mounds, up aloft, which are always very conspicuous, each branch bare of leaves, and according to its strength, holding smaller branches, covered with leafage with claw-like appearance as a curious effect. The Weeping Elm, in truth, is productive of capital results in scenery, when placed in situations adapted to its full display.

COLUMNAR TREES.

Trees of columnar form are of more weight in our decorations than is commonly supposed; and Nature, as if aware of this, has provided us with varieties adapted to scenes of many different characters. Too little, indeed, has been attempted in this country, in respect of the grouping of Columnar Trees. Objections are sometimes made, without any reasonable grounds, to having recourse to them. The aspect of a series of Lombardy Poplars is often vastly striking. I remember noticing an effect of this kind once, in the immediate neighbourhood of Worcester. Fewer mistakes in the employment of Columnar Trees would be made, if it were always borne in mind that they should be simply regarded as intensifying effects (or the strength of effects) in scenery. They exhibit, in truth, an infinite variety of massing from the erect acute to the most penduluous, as if calling for arrangements to suit them. Yet how often are they treated as though they all shared the characteristics of the Lombardy Poplar. Loudon, indeed, in his *Arboretum et Fruticetum Britannicum*, showed in what a variety of ways this tree (the Poplar) might be planted. And yet it only displays one out of the diversified conditions, which Columnar Trees are qualified to evince. Repton showed a scene in the front of his house improved by Columnar Poplar.

Some Columnar Trees are broadest at the base, while others, the *Cratægus Oxyacantha stricta* (Hawthorn), for example, evince an opposite tendency, increasing in breadth towards the summit. The genus *Cupressus* abounds in columnar plants, among others the delicate dark-hued *Cupressus Lawsoniana*, and its numerous distinct varieties. I have ventured to give figures of a few in the Plates 9, 10, and 11 of columnar plants.

PLATE 9

Cratægus Oxyacantha stricta

Quercus fastigiata

Populus fastigiata.

Pinus Laricio calabrica

The *Thuja occidentalis* is a tree of broad irregular columnar outline (see PLATE 10), and it preserves its breadth until quite near the summit. It has masses of beautiful light clouds of foliage, which, when touched with sunshine, display a sort of golden brown tint, very striking to look at in a good specimen and very distinct. The *Biota orientalis* has regular sharp outlines and sharp acute in its massings, while the leafage is of a lovely green. This genus, indeed, possesses many very effective members.

Juniperus.—The genus *Juniperus* contains many most charming plants ; no less than fifty varieties bearing this designation in our trade catalogues. Sometimes we hear complaints as to their not growing well, but if pleasure grounds were properly laid out, many different situations for the fostering of vegetation could be readily arranged. Various accounts have been published as to the conditions in which the Junipers flourish best; were these conditions, indeed, only sufficiently realised, it would establish a better basis for our operations, not only in respect of the *Juniperinæ*, but other plants requiring particular treatment as well. I have not myself, however, as yet, studied these growths sufficiently, so as to give a decided opinion on the subject ; nevertheless, I have seen specimens of Juniper which succeeded admirably in recesses made as though by accident, much surrounded by trees. They seem to like a good soil, free loam with natural drainage, as the side of some hill, thus possessing a continuous damp soil, and still not wet. The geographical distribution of the *Juniperæ* varies so much that it needs close and accurate observation to determine properly the right localities in which to place our specimens.

The Irish Juniper, *Juniperus communis hibernica*, is a shrub of columnar form. It presents a beautiful aspect when in vigorous growth, seeming as though it was a column composed of tips of silver. In many respects it well deserves our most sedulous care and attention. I have often witnessed this variety of Juniper thriving admirably in places like those which I have described. Most of the Junipers are of low stature, but some attain to an elevation of from thirty to forty feet.

The Irish Yew, *Taxus baccata fastigiata*, is a tree of the very darkest tint. When young it has a singular columnar outline, while afterwards it comes to display a number of spires in pure Gothic style.

These plants, when grouped, greatly contribute to a good display in our grounds. When fittingly arranged in some retired dell and surrounded by tall Firs, their influence on the mind is most impressive. The Yew may often be used with the best results in undulating scenery, and when placed at the lower end of a walk, will much enhance the lights and shades beyond.

Quercus pedunculata fastigiata, is as columnar as a Poplar, but has the angularity of the English Oak in the formation of the tree. See PLATE 9.

CONICAL OUTLINES.

The Austrian Pine, *Pinus austriaca*, assumes in its general outline a conical form. It is furnished with abundant, long irregular dark masses of foliage, which in the topmost branches oscillate with the breeze. This tree is well adapted for backgrounds, and yet it is injudicious to use it in preference to the *Pinus sylvestris*—a plant of the most lovely aspect. When sufficient space has been yielded for development, the *Pinus sylvestris* will become clothed with leafage almost to the very ground. The outlines are largest towards the base, and decrease towards the summit. The foliage displays the most decided undulations, while each several leaf seems to revel in the sun's light. When these Pines subsist together, the *Pinus sylvestris* appear to stand forth arrayed in all its beauty; while the *Pinus austriaca* seems to draw further back into its recess, showing how dissimilar are the plants, and how each is suited to its own particular place, giving an impression which is imparted by these trees for their respective effects.

The genus *Pinus* furnishes much variety in conical and other outlines. The characters noticed are to be found in plants which are spread over the country. In studying character of vegetation, it is of very little matter what forms are selected, for the observer must be able to read their feelings as he would a book; and when he can read the feelings given by vegetation, he will know something of arranging character. To know the place and its wants requires a true love for the art. Very many books might be written respecting character; but what the arranger must do will be to learn to read character in Nature herself, for without this he will be like a man commencing to read a book before he understands the letters.

PLATE 10

Biota orientalis.

Thuja occidentalis.

Cupressus macrocarpa.

Cupressus Lawsoniana.

CHAPTER VI.

OUTLINES.

THE principles of arrangement must be learned from Nature, for in Nature reside all beauty, all truth, and all excellence. Nevertheless, it is not everything witnessed in the multitudinous details of Nature that is to be copied, but only a select portion; and it is in this very selection, and the results flowing from it, that the whole art and mystery of gardening and beautifying of the landscape reside.

The proper arrangement of general outlines is one of the most important matters in the whole science of planting, for according as they are managed or mismanaged, will the pleasure or the opposite which flows from the treatment of the various characters of the vegetable world depend. As Trees and Shrubs cannot be so advantageously changed every day, general outlines, as far as possible, should take advantage of every beauty of the surrounding country. There must be a proper combination of favourable particulars, and an adequate adjustment of the different lines of sight. We shall have to plant according to the particular effects which we have in view, and the means and appliances which lie at our disposal. In the arrangement of parks and shrubberies, every natural feature and object, so far as possible, should be turned to account. Sometimes such features and such objects will be found adapted for bold display, while at other times they must be shut out. In short, we shall have to keep our particular intention continually in mind, and make our various dispositions accordingly.

As a general rule, the outlines of our gardens ought not to be planted with Forest Trees, unless indeed some sufficing reason for this subsist. Evergreens, Trees and Shrubs, should be employed in harmony with the scenery and the undulations of the soil, each plant in its place, and each supplying an effect. Too often, unfortunately, a very great absence of good taste is evidenced in the planting of trees. Some small piece of ground, it may be, consisting of a very few acres, is completely spoiled—for garden purposes at least—by being thickly covered by some half-dozen varieties of our ordinary Forest Trees; instead of each growth having sufficient space for the development of its beauty in unison with the scene. A garden, again, should display no abruptness. When it is found requisite to make breaks in masses of vegetation, these should be thinned out as they gain in dimension.

Few things in landscape are more calculated to occasion dissatisfaction than when we see the general outlines of decorated scenery occupied with perhaps three or four kinds of trees, each within a few feet of the other, and there left to become mere sticks, as it were, by reason of not having been thinned out at an early period of growth. A cruel contrivance, if I may employ such a term, is used to cover these so-called sticks—for example, a thick bank of shrubs placed in such wise that not more than about one-third of each shrub is visible; this is a falseness of arranging. To decorate, and then attempt to hide our decorations, does not seem a very satisfactory method. This is the cause of many a fair spot being void; this especially shows, in the first place as in the last, that an utter disregard and misconception of the principles of beauty are manifested. Procedures like this are much too general, thus making gardens bereft of life and beauty, which can be seen all over the country, not even excepting London.

Occasionally, sites of gardens and shrubbery grounds are bounded by a park, or, let us say, grass land, more or less undulated, or with adjoining hills. In such cases it will often be open to us very materially to improve the outlines before commencing to plant. Very often attempts are made to level soil at great expense, but this is a practice quite opposed to natural arrangements. Many a fair spot has been much injured by proceeding on such a system (wrong feeling), which does not suitably harmonise with the boundaries. As regards the contour of our grounds, among the first things to be thought of will be to turn to suitable account any recesses or hollows that may happen to subsist; to promote drainage, so as to prevent the ornamental grounds from showing little pools of water after every casual shower. The earth should not be placed in heaps, but left in natural undulations. Any surface, indeed, not absolutely level, will serve to maintain a tolerable dryness. In planting shrubs very often more land is attempted to be concealed than what is shown by the faulty dispositions of evergreens and other plants. Attempts are often made by means of evergreens to hide acres of ground, perhaps laid out at great expense, when the natural planting of such plants as *Rhododendron, Buxus*, or *Taxus*, in conjunction with the undulations of the soil, would have amply sufficed to conceal any undesirable view outside our grounds. (See Figure 3, Laws of Grouping and Natural Planting, page 40.) In case, indeed, the prospect were very objectionable, then walks might be lowered, and the soil itself next the boundaries raised. Lowering the ground in front of a border often imparts a sufficient elevation to the back, while the border hollows are well adapted to those growths to which a moist situation is congenial. In all our arrangements, in truth, every yard of soil should, so far as possible, be made to yield its quota of embellishment, and, as much as practicable, enhance the effect of our decorations.

How frequently does it happen when one goes to inquire why certain beautiful hardy forms are not oftener cultivated, one is referred to the bedding-out system, as though the ground in front of the drawing-room windows should comprise all our beautiful results, instead of having them distributed throughout the place. Hardy flowers, so termed, once thoroughly established, will often not require so much labour expended on them as is frequently lavished upon a well-kept Lawn.

By judicious arrangements, outlines might be rendered permanently attractive throughout the year. Outlines capable of greatly contributing to the character of each effect, are not always sufficiently turned to account. It is only by attending to details in subjection to some well designed general plan, that we can fill up our outlines, judiciously order our effects, and, in short, give Nature her due. In all our lines of sight, the ground line may be often undulated with vegetation three and four feet high, or even more in elevated countries, without destroying the lines of long distances. The want of some general principle of arrangement, as followed up in gardens, is evidenced by so often witnessing borders, flower-beds, groups of vegetable products, and single plants, all displayed irrespectively of each other. Such results are brought about by persons having a competent knowledge of the cultivation of some particular growths, perhaps with but little acquaintance with the laws which govern arrangement. The successful culture of flowers is one thing, but a knowledge of the disposition of plants, so as to produce effect, is another. The arranger, indeed, has to apply a knowledge of little use to a good working labourer, a knowledge which, if he even possess it, would soon be lost for want of use.

The centre of a garden, and of scenery generally, used often to be so elevated that little or no opportunity was left for developing extended views. Mr. Marnock, however, did much to discourage this system by his detailed design for flower-shows as displayed in the Regent's Park, thus showing that centres being kept low will bring a greater surface into sight than if the centre were kept high.

The various forms of vegetable growth should be so arranged as to render the results as pleasing as possible. Single plants ought not to form dots as it were, but should harmoniously unite with the scene around. Groups, indeed, should be in strictest unison with the outlying landscape. Masses ought in effect to strengthen the more precarious details, and, generally speaking, flower-beds and single plants alike must all combine to produce desirable permanent results. (See all PLATES given, their Outlines and Centres.)

Desirable combinations are not to be attained by planting points here and there, showing, perhaps, but a third of our shrubs, or in the mere levelling of soil. Each subject of the scene must fulfil its part, and adequately contribute to the harmony of the whole.

The recesses and vistas that gardens after the Dutch manner displayed, have been done away with, and nothing, so to speak, has replaced them; and yet recesses and vistas far more beautiful might abound in our pleasure grounds, were we only to follow Nature's guidance in forming natural outlines, and planting proportion of various lines of sight together, according to the style of the scenery. Summer and winter effects might be more satisfactorily developed than they are, if only the climate were turned to better account, and the resources that our plants furnish were rendered of more avail.

Every effect may be said to have its scene and outlines, although no division appears, or should appear, between the two, but both should unite together as the leaves of a tree group together into masses, producing also the general outline of the tree. A great general principle to attain in arrangement is, how to make the garden beautiful all the year round—that is, both in winter and summer— and by arranging the scenery according to the outlines and its scene, you have already formed two divisions of effect in general, the first for winter, and the second for summer results.

To accomplish a moderate share of outlines, the beauty of each plant must be seen; for if you have shrubs, you should have not only these, but carpeting plants and trees, or else you cannot give satisfactory effects to the outlines of the scene. By referring merely to the outlines given in Figure 1, PLATE 3, page 40, any one may conceive the ruinous effects of that style of arrangement being carried out by placing plants all of one size together, and massed in such quantities as form one void surface from the water's edge, out of all proportion to ground and the form of the vegetation used. Instead of this, every line of sight should have its due proportion of the effects in accordance with its style to produce the harmony required by the mind. These undulations may appear confusion to the learner; but he will never become competent to arrange truly, until he sees clearly what is necessary to complete their beauties—mystery without confusion.

In formal gardening, plants are at present used to break the monotony of the level effects, these possessing more or less the size of shrubs, giving light and shade, as well as increasing the outlines of the effects, in accordance with their arrangement, being more or less satisfactory, as they fulfil the wants of the effects to the beauty already arranged, by being in true proportion and unification with the scene and its surroundings. In dividing these formal gardens, or other ground for planting, for winter and summer effects, the edgings of the beds, consisting of permanent plants, should form features of beauty in themselves for winter effects, as well as form bases to assist the development of the brighter effects of summer. It may be seen, to accomplish this, that the edgings must not be mere lines of one plant or another, but form margins, to the effects in true proportion of the designs. These plants, as well as carpeting the ground, should have bulbs and other plants springing from their midst in groups of bright flowers in due course.

In natural planting, the bold outlines produce promontories and recesses, each of these possessing various degrees of importance, all different from each other, but still all combining to develop the scenery in course of arrangement. Some of these are shown in the various examples of the outlines given in PLATES 2, 3, 4, 5, 6, 7, and 8, for the centres and outlines of scenery. All outlines of scenery, however, should be arranged to develop the natural effects of the land and vegetation, in accordance with the requirements of the style placed upon the ground.

Amongst these many undulating outlines, it will be seen at once that some promontories and recesses, even in the ground plans given, are features of the principal effects of the scenery and others belonging to the more local displays, thus forming local and principal effects. By examining the principal or local outlines, it will be seen that each again has its general and detailed effects in the before-mentioned promontories and recesses, these forming great varieties of sites, suitable for the development of the various forms of vegetation that the climate may grow, for which the arrangement is made.

In considering the forms of vegetation, as productive of good results, both evergreen and deciduous plants should have a just proportion of their effects in nearly all scenery. Nevertheless, in general, but not absolutely, both have their proper place in the arrangements to be the principle thereof. Before proceeding further, I venture to remark that very qualifying terms are necessary for producing effective scenery—for example, however beautiful scenery is made it can be enjoyed more from beneath the deep shadow of some gigantic umbrageous tree than standing out in the open light; and thus for this reason and others, scenery gives power to the arranger to make every line of sight complete. The tree planted in the foreground for its shade can be made to assist the development of the scenery by becoming often a principle in the general outlines from other distances and sites.

In returning to our former subject—the examining of outlines, the general effects spoken of, which might be called the general promontories, require to be more or less permanent in their results, and thereby planted with plants giving effects, particularly during the winter division of the year. These will also produce a summer effect. They should of necessity be usually evergreen, but both the deciduous and evergreen must complete their effects according to the laws of massing and extent, entwining each other in a limited manner, to complete the scenery accordingly.

In speaking of the chief sites for deciduous plants, these may be broadly stated to be the recesses and detail promontories.

When every plant, or group of plants, forms a feature of itself and a part of the scenery, it is surprising how few plants will warm the scene and complete the effects, even in the dullest period of winter. The Laws of Massing and Extent, shown in PLATE 3, page 40, will be found of use as a base to the thoughts in arranging outlines.

In studying the advantages of undulations, many great features soon develop themselves to the mind, giving power to complete effects to satisfaction. The three lines of sight mentioned contain many other subordinate parts, which can be seen in any arrangement of plant life.

In arranging for perpetual effect, a base to each of the three lines of sight will be advantageous, particularly for deciduous scenes. A base is formed by planting the first perceptible variation of the principal line of sight, with some plant producing permanent effects in proportion to the outlines of the scenery—for example, in the ground line of sight such plants as some of the genera *Saxifraga*, *Sedum*, *Pernettya*, *Erica*, *Vaccinium*, *Gaultheria*, *Andromeda*, *Menziesia*, and *Cotoneaster*. For the larger growths in the middle and higher lines of sight, shrubs in the prominences of the masses can also be arranged with advantage for the same end.

In placing the front of the prominences with plants giving a base to masses of vegetation around, it may surprise some how little ground is occupied to apparently form a base for quantities of vegetation beyond, and showing forth their effects for general admiration.

When consulted respecting a Park of many acres, I was requested to arrange it so as to have a more evergreen effect, as the proprietor usually occupied this residence in the winter. There was also pointed out to me a single Portugal Laurel, with the remark, "See how that single shrub warms the effect of the whole of the deciduous trees around, upon this winter's day." And such was the fact. By properly placing a few plants, deciduous scenes can be made to have a beauty in winter.

CHAPTER VII.

TIME—SUITABLY DIVIDED FOR PERPETUAL BEAUTY.

TIME, which so powerfully influences affairs here below, exercises an agency of the very greatest moment in all decorative efforts. Vegetable products vary most materially at the different periods of their existence. The *Cedrus Libani*, for example, has a spiral form of growth in its early days, and gains a sort of table-shaped summit when it reaches maturity. Many plants are effective only during a few months, while others are so throughout the entire twelve. Time, indeed, must be taken into consideration in every arrangement which we may happen to make. Wait, only wait, and often, as through a species of magic, results ensue which were the least hoped for, and as charming as they are unexpected.

In all our operations the various so-termed Permanent Plants must prove the basis. Ever-bounteous Nature has provided these sufficingly for every display, the flowers taking precedence in Summer, and the fruitage in Autumn.

When the period of each plant's life comes to a close, another plant should be coming forward to occupy its place. In general we should so order our operations that each season may manifest a beauty of its own. Many vegetable forms yield effects for so very brief a period that it needs care to replace them by others of a more durable kind.

In studying how we may render our grounds beautiful, not for months only, but for years, it will be necessary to have recourse to means adapted to the end. Some growths endure but for a season, while others last for whole hundreds of years. Three points demand our closest attention in respect of planting—permanency of effects, future effects, and present effects.

Many plants do not show their fullest beauty until touched by the hand of Time—for example, the British oak, *Quercus pedunculatus, Cedrus Libani, Taxus baccata,* and others. In arranging these long-lived growths, their after effects, which must prove an after effect to us, have to be most attentively considered. Indeed, certain examples give us a sort of foretaste of the pleasure which is to fall to the lot of others. Trees such as these strike even the most careless with admiration, and are worthy of a lasting place in our regards. They do not, in the first instance at least, interfere with any of our other combinations; and as they require but a small amount of space in their early days, may thus always form a portion of the scenery. As they should be generally planted at long distances apart, ample scope will be commonly left for developing other and subsequent effects.

What I would term future or prospective effects are not always held of sufficient account. Many plants do not begin to develop their character of beauty until perhaps some ten or twenty years have elapsed. Mistakes are made in reference to this matter, and not discovered before it proves almost too late to rectify them. Unremitting attention and care, always bearing in mind the successes which our growths are intended to achieve, can alone ensure us success. Plants used for present purposes can be removed in due course as the more permanent ones gain in dimension. A season before removal, their roots ought to be prepared in the usual way.

In respect of the treatment of Trees and Shrubs, proper thinning out is too frequently neglected. How often, in gardens, do we see Portugal and other Laurels which have quite ruined Yews and Hollies. Were such matters seen to in proper time, they might be obviated, and short-lived and quick-growing shrubs would not then be allowed to injure plants of a more permanent description. The duration of plants, to whatever class they may happen to belong, holds an important place in our arrangements, for trees and shrubs of the longest endurance are most worthy of the highest rank in our esteem; and there will always be enough room left for present effects when preparations are made for these two after effects.

The space lying between the back outlines and the foreground of our landscape ought, in general, to be allotted to growths that display effects during the summer period. The outlines of foreground and background, on the other hand, should be occupied by plants giving permanent display, more especially in winter. All our planting, indeed, must have an object in view. Each effect, in order to achieve beautiful results, must be complete in itself. In this we only follow the order pursued by Nature. A mound of undulating outlines, suitably decorated, will present attractions, each succeeding the other, throughout the whole course of the year. As for the general outlines, they may be completed by the introduction of permanent plants, giving successional effects six winter months of the year, and forming most beautiful outlines for summer. Special results are best realised in all their glory by availing ourselves of the attractions of plants in succession after succession, singly or in groups, each complete in itself.

In studying effective arrangements, nothing, comparatively speaking, will be found so desirable as to make use of plants that will bear the vicissitudes of our climate. In other respects, a splendid display in autumn can alone be achieved by resorting to tender plants; but, by proper proportions of outlines and mid-lines of sight, beautified by hardy plants, a far greater brilliancy could be given in autumn; and, on the whole, a natural and permanent beauty must be principally sought for by resorting to plants which our climate is capable of developing. This premised, we must seek for those forms and colours in vegetation that will yield an outcome at every period of the year. Of course, as I have said before, we must resort for decoration to tender flowers in autumn; but for permanent results, winter and summer, we shall perforce have recourse to hardy forms of vegetation. I would therefore separate the periods of growth into two great divisions, one suitable for winter, the other for summer. This will be found best adapted to the natural arrangement and harmonious combination which ought to subsist in all scenery. At the same time, there ought to subsist a continuity between both of these divisions, so that there shall be no abrupt line of demarcation between the two. Many of our Rhododendrons, indeed, will often yield a considerable display at both periods of the year. In fact, we are not to be bound too strictly by square and line, but should endeavour to blend our harmonies by conforming to Nature's laws, according to the facilities at our disposal. Some plants better fulfil these objects at different periods of flowering than do others—for example, the *Arabis albida* will remain effective for six months at a time, while other plants will endure far less a period of time with their flowers. This division, with those named in the last chapter, taking into account the availability of the soil, will, I think, fulfil our objects better, and prove more productive of plant beauty than any other.

When summer's reign is over, it is then that we begin most fully to appreciate the beauty of our evergreen plants. With all their varying lights and shades they embellish our pleasure grounds, soften to us the rigours of the season, until spring shall return, laden with treasures, in order to scatter them in rich profusion at the very foot of man. Summer shines throughout with a yet more glowing radiance than the spring. The brilliancy with which she clothes the earth, the enchanting fragrance which she scatters broadcast, the soft haze with which she veils the landscape, the sunny beauty of her skies. Closely following summer's footsteps autumn comes, bearing richest fruits, touching as with a magic wand the trees that presently are to glow with many a wondrous tint of crimson, and of gold, and of scarlet.

There are various natural scenes which show forth beauties from early spring till latest autumn without any assistance from art. Some old Hawthorn hedge, for example, will display a pleasant bordering of early Primroses and Violets, and, when May arrives, wraps itself over with fair sweet flowers. Then the Wild Rose peeps forth with her lovely delicate buds, and in autumn Rose and Thorn alike vie with each other in bright array of scarlet fruitage—a perfect delight to look at—yielding a regale for the birds in requital of their songs. Yet many a scene would manifest results not less charming than these would we only avail ourselves of Nature's guidance; but, led astray by technical principles, we fail to understand, and miss the pleasures which otherwise we might enjoy.

We frequently see groups of Thorns or other trees with hardly anything but grassy space around them. Grass, in its various forms, what a blessing to mankind it has proved. Nevertheless, it is not desirable to employ invariably one kind of grass in our arrangements, or occupy with it the entire arena of any scene. It will, in most cases, be rendered more effective by the adjunct of various other carpeting plants, as in Nature. There may be connected with the trees, by intermediate growths, shrubs, for example, and the like. Nature garlands her trees in the most lovely fashion with climbing plants—a decoration in which we may invest when we will.

This earth which we inhabit provides us with the sustenance which we need. But it does something far transcending this. Numberless, indeed, are the sources of knowledge, of delight, of love with which it everywhere abounds; numberless, in truth, as are the

M

sands on the shores of the great deep itself. The earth is to many like an unexplored country, the mysterious recesses of which they have never striven to penetrate. A boundless kingdom of beauty, if only we had eyes wherewith to see it, stretches around us on every hand; a well-spring of joy, which subsists till earth's loveliness pales around us, and another life begins. It is said that at the sight of the Apollo Belvidere, the human body involuntarily erects itself, and assumes a more lofty attitude. And thus it is with objects which inspire us with just and true perceptions, elevate our moral nature, purify the heart. There seems, indeed, a sort of kinship between beauty and goodness, and where the one is we would fain discover the other also. Alas, it is not always thus!

Let us, then, strive to render our landscapes beautiful year by year—nay, rather day by day. Let us avoid, too, many changes. If ground be properly laid out, these will seldom prove needful; and should it, in any case, be found desirable to add new features this should be done as much as possible without disturbing older ones. We occasionally hear evergreens objected to, as possessing, so to speak, too serious an aspect. But if fittingly arranged, the effects produced with their aid may be soft or bright at pleasure. They are not only lovely in themselves, but often alike afford shelter to other plants from winter's blast or summer's scorching ray. It is astonishing what a large number of growths there are that continue to gladden us throughout the year. Many of the very noblest forms of vegetation are evergreen, and some of these—the *Cedrus Libani*, for example—are covered with a profusion of flowers in the early winter months, as may be witnessed at Dropmore and other places. It is, perhaps, during this occasionally rather dreary period that evergreens appear to give us the greatest amount of pleasure. They shine brightly forth amid November's mists, seeming to gain fresh lustre from the moisture which envelops them. Should frost arrive, they will then be laden with glittering masses of exquisite beauty, the long, dark extended branches, as in the case of our larger firs, contrasting most strikingly with the stainless whiteness of the new fallen snow. Evergreen are nearly the principal effects during nine months of the year.

I am of opinion that were the outlines already named in our shrubberies and gardens more generally planted with a view to winter effects, it would lead us thus to the introduction of many growths most suitable for our purposes in foregrounds as well as backgrounds. I remember seeing in a nursery bed some seedling *Pernettya mucronata*, with beautifully varied berries in many different hues. But in Nature there is a rich abundance of structures adapted for our uses to show forth various feelings of character, were we only to arrange them harmoniously and well. As I have oftener than once already observed, we might so arrange that our gardens should yield a rich display throughout the whole course of the year, one period of the year always, as it were, predominant, another subservient, but uniting so as to enhance the pleasing aspect of our grounds. As regards carpeting plants, a very small space indeed, will sometimes suffice to yield the most charming results. The so-termed foliage plants often attain sufficient elevation to justify their adoption as a background for carpeting plants, or to fill up recesses, vistas, and the like. This term, carpeting plants, I have ventured to apply to those various small growths that do, indeed, make it their principle object to carpet the ground. The name includes Alpine plants, herbaceous, rock, bedding plants, and many others ; for the convenience of speaking upon all these low growths at once, of course, using other terms for particular forms when wanted. Too often these are, as it were, dotted over with the surface, instead of covering it as in Nature. If we have only enough for mere specks, it would be better to hold them in reserve until we had wherewithal to suffice, and had ascertained by observation the best situation in which to place them. There are, indeed, many herbaceous growths that would hold out most agreeably for a term of three years or even a much longer period, as may be witnessed throughout Nature's fair abodes. In other respects, a provision may be made for such plants as require to be handled in some particular manner.

Endeavours are sometimes made in flower gardens to supplement the deficiency in winter brightness by having resort to bulbs, shrubs, coloured minerals, and such like, as occupying the space usually filled by flowers in summer. Such results, however, should not be aimed at in too direct contravention of natural arrangements. They may sometimes prove desirable in contiguity to a mansion or buildings where the outlines in winter foregrounds do not yield perfect satisfaction.

Those plants that are productive of effects throughout the entire year, are most justly subjects of admiration. The *Rhododendron*, before commented on—the *Ilex*, the *Berberis*, the *Arbutus*—all enchant us with their flowers and fruitage alike, while smaller growths of many and various kinds can be had recourse to in furtherance of our designs, and, when not in their special effect, give a base to the beauty of other growths.

Nature's operations are at once ever beautiful and ever sure. They repose on a basis firm as is the structure of the globe itself. Every plant we make the object of study is found to display a beauty of youth, of maturity, and of decline. The tender grass renders our valleys replete with verdure; the clustering Ivy hangs on many a tree; while in sequestered shady nooks lurk mosses and graceful ferns. Many a hilly tract is covered by the heather, and far-extending slopes by the majestic Pine. High up on mountain sides peep forth sweet Alpine flowers, snow-protected during the greater portion of the year, and perfect miracles of loveliness in spring.

We do not soon tire of plants that display beauties which are rare at the season in which they appear. The Snowdrop, for example, Crocus, Scilla, Violet, Anemone, Daphne, and the Hepatica, are all effective in the extreme, and can be disposed so as not to interfere with other combinations. The *Erica herbacea curnea* flowers from November till April. It is, therefore, excellent as a plant wherewith to form a ground to other plants. Its masses of dark green foliage can be developed well in summer with the hues of other prevailing growths. Grasses of various outlines impart an agreeable diversity. We need not always have recourse to ordinary grasses when so many other kinds subsist—such as the *Festuca ovina*, the *Carex pendula*, and the lovely *Gynerium argenteum* (Pampas grass) of Buenos Ayres.

The Vincas, more especially the varieties of *Vinca minor*, are very serviceable in places otherwise too dry for grass. In some such I have seen the blue and white flowers of both green-leaved varieties and variegated subsist the winter through. Ivies, which Nature well knows how to handle, can be so disposed, both as regards outline and hue, as to suit every curvature of the soil for covering land. As a ground for other effects, Ferns, in shady dells and hollows where sufficient moisture abounds, most agreeably cover the soil. The *Cotoneaster microphylla* affords a good dark basis for other displays, and will furnish us with white flowers in spring, and scarlet berries in autumn time. Many varieties of the well-known *Cydonia*, which has fine early flowers, and subsequently very curious fruitage, is well adapted for covering quantities of wild, warm banks, and other scenery. The different kinds of *Amygdalus*, although not permanent effective plants, might be much more extensively cultivated than they at present are. They can be planted with the greatest advantage in recesses and places not too conspicuous. And when their beautiful flowers appear, they claim a very high place in our estimation as harbingers of spring.

The various special beauties of a scene should succeed each other, so as not to destroy one another's effects by coming in opposition or together. As all outlines govern the scene, they should at all times possess an effect of their own, and also should be suitable for making all their various special effects, each and all complete, in their respective seasons. Even deciduous scenes require some plants of an evergreen character, not only to assist their winter's effect, but to assist their development, and to impress their effects on the mind. Therefore, when this is so, it may be said that the boundary outlines of scenery will always require assistance, more or less, from permanent plants, either in the foreground or background of the scenes or outlines, or in both. Many books and catalogues enumerate the varieties of permanent plants, necessary for forming outlines and bases to scenery, as well as giving particular beauties of their own, varying in all sizes, from forms just vailing the earth to giants of majesty; and in the same sources of information, the less permanent varieties of effective plants, which are more or less temporary in their beauties, will be found noticed. All effects can receive full justice, both for their growth and effects in the natural arrangement without destroying the permanency of the general results.

The equality or repetition given in technical art is completely out of place in Nature's effect. In the undulation of vegetation and land, ever varying forms succeed each other in succession, all in perfect balance and proportion, so that each plant, or group of plants, is complete within itself, and still lends its quota to the maintaining of the general effects, without any apparent division; group succeeding group producing infinite beauty throughout the periods of the year, in the numerous lines of sight. It will surprise those who have not arranged for perpetual beauty, how very few groups in the various lines of sight forms a base, and gives a permanent character, leaving room for any object wanted. These bases should principally form part of the outlines or winter's division of effects. The following tables may assist some to divide their special effects into suitable periods:—

TABLE OF SPECIAL EFFECTS OF TREES AND SHRUBS.

WINTER DIVISION.		
Oct., Nov., and Dec.	Dec., Jan., and Feb.	Feb., Mar., and April.
Pyrus, scarlet berries Salix, of sorts * Betula, various * Cedrus Libani	Evergreens are now the principal effects, and possess many distinctive beauties.	Amygdalus cochinchinensis Persica, of sorts [April Sambucus, golden foliage in Acer, do. Populus, do.
Arbutus, of sorts (P) Garrya, of sorts (P) Azalea Ghent varieties [Scarlet Althæa frutex leaves] Coronilla Emerus Monthly Roses	Laurustinus Jasminum nudiflorum Andromeda, of sorts (P) Corchorus japonica *	Abelia floribunda Berberis, of sorts (P) Uydonia japonica Forsythia Furze Daphne, of sorts Mahonia, of sorts (P) Ribes, of sorts Persica, of sorts

SUMMER DIVISION.	
May, June, and July.	July, Aug., and Sept.
Robinia, of sorts Cratægus, of sorts (E) Cytisus Laburnum Pyrus Ancuparia (Mountain Ash) Æsculus Hippocastanum	True effects, even now, receive great assistance from Evergreen forms.
Andromeda, of sorts (P) Amorpha fruticosa Azalea (hardy) Buddlea globosa Ceanothus, of sorts Clematis, of sorts Colutea, of sorts Coronilla Cytisus, of sorts Genista, of sorts Deutzia, of sorts Pyracantha (P) Philadelphus, of sorts Pæonia, Tree Syringa, of sorts (Lilac) Sambucus, of sorts Spiræa, of sorts Rhododendron (P) Rosa, of sorts Lonicera, of sorts (Honeysuckle)	Abelia rupestris, J. to Dec. ———— uniflora. Clethra arborea Althæa frutex (in September) Genista sibirica and tinctoria Leycesteria formosa Hydrangea Spiræa, of sorts Clematis, of sorts Passiflora, of sorts

Names marked thus (*) continue their effects until May.   (P) means permanent or evergreen.

TABLE OF SPECIAL EFFECTS OF CARPETING PLANTS.

WINTER DIVISION.

Oct., Nov., and Dec.	Dec., Jan., and Feb.	Feb., Mar., and April.
Erica herbacea carnea*	The beautiful early leaves of—	Erica mediterranea
Chrysanthemum	Aquilegia, of sorts	Anemone, of sorts*
Vinca minor*	Aconitum, of sorts	Hepatica, of sorts*
—— minor alba*	Centaurea montana	Polygala Chamæbuxus
Rosa	Lupinus, of sorts	Iris reticulata
Agapanthus umbellatus	Verbascum Thapsus	Aubrietia deltoidea
Aster, of sorts	Pæonia, of sorts*	Tulipa, of sorts*
Primula* { Polyanthus	Ferula Ferulago	Myosotis, of sorts*
{ Primroses	The Flowers of— [drops]	Gentiana acaulis*
Bellis (Dble. Daisies)	Galanthus nivalis (Snow-	Lithospermum prostratum
Viola (Pansy)	Eranthis hyemalis	Omphalodes verna
—— Trentham blue*	(Winter Aconite)	Corydalis, of sorts
—— Trentham yellow*	Helleborus niger	Alströmeria caryophylles
—— (Violets) Czar*	Arabis albida	Ranunculus amplexicaulis
Tritoma Uvaria	Antennaria* margaritacea	Arabis albida*
Gynerium argenteum	(the leaves)	Scilla, of sorts* [Tooth Violet]
	Tussilago fragrans	Erythronium dens canis (Dog-
		Muscari, of sorts
Names marked thus (*) continue their effects until May.		Fritillaria, of sorts

SUMMER DIVISION.

May, June, and July.	July, Aug., and Sept.
Cistus	Erica cinerea
Helianthemum	Erica coccinea
Erica multiflora alba	Erica Tetralix pallida
—— multiflora rubra	Erica vagans
Pyrethrum, of sorts	Potentilla, of sorts
Viola, of sorts	Polygonum, of sorts
Pæonia, of sorts	Bedding plants
Dianthus, various	Annuals
Linum, of sorts	Hollyhocks
Phlox, of sorts (Alpine)	Lobelia, herbaceous varieties
Polemonium, of sorts	Tradescantia, of sorts
Papaver, of sorts	Oxalis lasiandra
Lupinus, of sorts	Campanula, of sorts
Cheiranthus alpinus	Anchusa semperflorens
Hieracium, of sorts (P), cover the ground from weeds	Pentstemon, of sorts
Trollius (golden cups of flowers in May)	Phlox, of sorts
Veronica spicata	Astrantia, of sorts
Lilium undulatum (scarlet)	Verbascum, of sorts
Orobus atropurpureus (dark)	Veronica, of sorts
Œnothera, of sorts	Salvia, of sorts
Funkia, of sorts	Arundo conspicua
Hemerocallis, of sorts	Scabiosa, of sorts
Lilium, of sorts	Antennaria margaritacea
Iris, of sorts	Linum, of sorts
Asphodelus, of sorts	Coreopsis, of sorts
Convallaria, (Lily of the valley)	Calliopsis, of sorts
Hesperis, of sorts	Helianthus
Iberis, of sorts	Lilium, of sorts
	Czackia Liliastrum
	Epilobium, of sorts
	Funkia subcordata
	Colchicum, of sorts
	Digitalis, of sorts
	Statice, of sorts
	Stipa pennata
	Spiræa filipendula
	Gunnera, of sorts
	Lathyrus, of sorts
	Monarda, of sorts
	Lythrum, of sorts

AUTUMN EFFECTS.

The hues worn by the trees in autumn have already been alluded to. The Maples, Scarlet Oak *(Quercus coccinea)*, and others, assume the very richest tints. As on a soft bright day we survey some woodland scene, bathed in golden sunshine, with leafage all aglow, it would almost seem as though some high festival of Nature were in preparation to celebrate the happy fruitions of the year.

Different varieties of what are termed Ghent Azaleas, imparta very pleasing autumnal warmth by their leaves giving a bright scarlet; while among others the Althæa frutex displays its pretty blossoms, even as late as October and November.

The Rose, commonly termed Monthly Rose, in mild seasons and in sheltered situations, will yield abundant flowers throughout October, November, December, and January. In most gardens a place suitable for these plants can be found. It will often prove advantageous to have some early Chrysanthemums, in spots not too conspicuous, however. Large groups of *Tritoma Uvaria* afford an excellent display, and, when in good condition, the foliage proves effective during a great portion of the year. The flowers themselves, indeed, are very handsome, and often a single plant will present as many as thirty spikes at one and the same time. Many places may be suitably occupied by these plants, which harmonise well with more permanent growths. The *Viburnum Tinus*, the *Andromeda floribunda*, and others assist the autumn and winter effects.

The coloured stems of some trees, the *Salices*, for example, and the *Betula alba*, often help to brighten our winter landscape. The scarlet Dogwood *(Cornus alba)*, is excellent in park scenery. There are very good masses of this plant at Caledon Park, Armagh. The *Deutzia crenata flore-pleno* has a pale yellowish bark in winter, and much variety in this respect subsists amongst deciduous growths. The *Jasminum nudiflorum* are of great importance as regards the winter effects of climbers.

MID-WINTER EFFECTS.

The months of December, January, and February need not prove so deficient in the matter of flowers, as to the general aspect of gardens at this season might imply. Not very much or various choice have we, it is true; still enough subsists wherewith to enable us to create a most agreeable diversity. Nor need these winter arrangements interfere with later ones. In sheltered spots a number of plants will thrive throughout most winters, and, should an exceptionally severe season ensue, and they should run any risk of perishing, we can always yield them sufficient protection. Generally speaking, however, the ground, when properly handled, will afford the best shelter. Plants, again, when arranged according to natural exigencies, do much to shield and protect one another. But tender plants, of small size, exposed in our grounds in winter, often require—and, indeed, imperatively demand—as much heedful care as do our Geraniums within doors.

As already said, I have watched the unfolding of the white and blue flowers of *Vinca minor*, and *Vinca minor alba*, from autumn until late in spring. The *Viola odorata Czar*, Trentham Blue, and Trentham Yellow Pansies, and *Tussilago fragrans*, quite surprise and enchant us with their early vernal visitation. In sheltered spots, indeed, numerous plants display their flowers throughout the winter months —namely, the Wall-flower, *Cheiranthus Cheiri*, many kinds of *Primula* (Polyanthuses and Primroses), with varieties of the *Bellis* (Double Daisies). There are, again, growths which exhibit their beautiful leafage even in the month of January. Such are various forms of *Aquilegia* (leaves coming like Roses), *Lupinus, Aconitum, Centaurea montana, Antennaria margaritacea* (like tips of snow), and others. Many varieties of *Ferula* and *Arums* deserve attention, as also various herbaceous Pæonies, with their ruddy leaves, with foliage as bright as the *Irisine*, at a later period. The dark evergreen foliage of the Christmas Rose, or *Helleborus niger*, used in proper proportion, will much enhance many winter effects. The garden must indeed be small where some few square yards of space cannot be conceded for such subjects as these. Though not very exacting in respect of nourishment, they can often be seen doing well in a poor, dry soil. The *Eranthis hyemalis* (the Winter Aconite), even in early January, will often be covered with a perfect profusion of golden flowers. And along with the flowers of autumn and winter effects come the Berry-bearing plants, which impart a very pleasing aspect. Were we, in truth, but so minded, our grounds in winter might yield very many more effects than what is commonly the case.

SPRING EFFECTS.

The *Cerasus Padus* (Bird Cherry) has a fine white display of flowers in April and May. Varieties of *Persica* and *Mespilus* prove charming, small-sized, early flowering trees. Then, to speak of shrubs, we have the *Abelia floribunda*, many kinds of *Berberis* and *Daphne*, the golden-flowered *Forsythia viridissima*, and *F. suspensa*, and the *Andromeda*. The *Cydonia japonica* is an extremely handsome plant, producing an abundance of scarlet or white flowers in this division. It admits of being trained into the most formal shapes, so as to suit an Italian garden. Its curious autumnal fruitage harmonises well with the quaint architectural recess. Many varieties of *Cydonia* do best in sheltered portions of the shrubbery, where they often assume the most fantastic forms. One of the best known and generally admired among our shrubs is the *Ribes*, or Flowering Currant. Many an otherwise uninteresting spot it might serve to embellish. The leaves, which appear very early, last till the frost removes them, and then the stems often exhibit a cheerful bright red tint. I have seen some of these plants cut down by frost in exceptionally severe winters, when perhaps but a few yards off there would, in some sheltered nook, be found others fifteen feet in height, or even more.

There are various growths which might be arranged so as most beneficially to occupy the ground and foregrounds, and many of these might be so disposed as to grow up through small carpeting plants, grouped according to character. Such are Crocuses, Snowdrops, Hepaticas, Anemones, *Iris reticulata*, Tulips, *Scilla;* while such as the *Myosotis, Gentiana acaulis*, the beautiful blue *Omphalodes verna*, and others, would form carpeting groups themselves. The numerous kinds of Primrose and Polyanthus constitute a perfect delight in the spring by the abundance of their flowers, and, when the summer comes, their leaves often serve as a capital margin. The *Cheiranthus alpinus* produces an excellent effect in spring, and the curious evergreen leaves are often serviceable as arranged with other plants. The *Phloxes* possess many beautiful effects—*P. divaricata*, for example, has beautiful pale blue flowers. Many other plants there are, however, which I have not enumerated, but which might be grown with every advantage during the early months of the year.

Snowdrops, as well as other bulbous growths, can be planted

in abundance midst the grass of shrubberies and parks, and round borders and beds, in more formal arrangements, and this without interfering in the least with the occupants of the soil. Indeed, we can always prevent their being injured by any digging operations. It would prove very desirable were these growths permitted a longer period—say a week or a fortnight—in order to ripen their foliage. Were this done, a greater number of bulbs and finer flowers would prove the result, than when the leaves are allowed to be cut off before being dead. The *Erythronium dens canis* will show itself most serviceable when not interfered with. I once saw a very fine display of this plant growing on a long bank of grass under trees. It was always left to take care of itself, as I was told by Major Waring, on whose property it grew at Waringstown. The *Iris reticulata* is an early flowering bulbous plant, not sufficiently cultivated. Anemones, again, would cover with great advantage much of the apparently barren ground which gardens are wont to exhibit in the early season of the year.

Many of the plants that bloom early will continue to display their flowers, such, for example, as the *Arabis*, *Myosotis*, and others. The beautiful effects of Horse Chesnuts, *Æsculus Hippocastanum*, at this period, have always been justly admired. Perhaps among the noblest specimens of these trees are those witnessed in the Chesnut Avenue at Bushey Park. They are commonly found to sustain very strong blasts, indeed; but the delicate *Acacia*, which begins to flower much about the same time, will need very careful and tender handling to select a place sheltered from wind. In return, it will richly reward us with its graceful leafage, and flowers of many a hue. The different species of *Cratægus*, *Syringa*, and also the *Cytisus* (Laburnum), are very lovely objects when fittingly displayed. Later in the season, we have roses which, with their rich variety of tints, prove perfect fountains alike of beauty and of perfume. Many hardy specimens of Azaleas unfold their flowers early in summer, as likewise plants belonging to the following genera—to wit, *Ceanothus*, *Clematis*, *Kalmia*, *Buddlea*, *Sambucus*, *Lonicera*, late varieties of *Ribes*, *Spiræa*, *Jasminum*, and *Philadelphus*. Place for these—and many more besides can be found in a garden of very moderate dimensions—in the outlines of the scenes, without in any way interfering with other or subsequent effects. Again, the Tulip produces a perfectly ravishing display. Gesner, who was the first to make it known by his botanical description and figure, saw it in 1559, at Augsburg, the seeds having been brought there from the Levant. In the middle of the seventeenth century, Tulips became objects of an unprecedented commerce, their prices in many instances rising above that of the precious metals themselves. That exquisite flower, the Rose, has been the emblem of England now for well nigh four hundred years, while, on the other hand, the Lily has been chosen to represent France. The varieties of *Viola tricolor*, commonly termed Heartsease, and those of the *Dianthus*, so well known as Carnations, Picotees, and Pinks, are perfect beauties in their own character, and, so far as they extend, perennial incentives to the cultivation of human worth and excellence. " I often think," observes Miss Mitford in her admirable letters, " that of all as shown to us in this beautiful world, that little world of flowers in its sweetness and innocence and peace, is the truest and best example of what we ought to try to be ourselves—opening our hearts, as best we may, to the bright sunshine and the pure air of heaven, and sweetening and beautifying to our fellow-creatures the path of life along which we dwell."

Book III.—Principal Effects and Styles of Scenery.

CHAPTER I.
SCENERY—PRINCIPLES.

I shall now endeavour to set forth, in a general way, a few of the practical bearings of the subjects already adverted to ; and thus, as far as may be, render assistance to those who may take pleasure in the important art of landscape arrangement. Extended landscapes vary greatly according as they are looked at from a high or a low point of view. It will be needful, therefore, to consider sites in connection with the positions, from which they are commonly to be looked at. In the case of natural depressions, the land will often be found occupied by water, which will allow many effects to become conspicuous. As regards a high ground, on the other hand, the opposite holds good ; for here the principal centre will generally subsist wherever the surface is highest. In a hilly country, indeed, we shall commonly find that a single elevation is, as it were, the *point de mire* of the entire prospect.

I had some intention originally of giving in these pages plans of what might be called perpetual gardens; but when I thought upon the host of garden plans in every horticultural publication, I refrained from doing so: for, however beautiful, some particular effects are produced on paper, or in some gardens, say those of Kew, they are carried away and mutilated by persons who do not bestow thought upon their suitability for their object, thus transforming designs of beauty into forms which are disgusting. At present, therefore, I have confined myself to one object — the principles of arrangement; and, I will venture to state, that if they were more studied, the deplorable results of beauty spoiled and money wasted would not be so frequent, as every first-class horticulturist knows them to be, too often, at present. The landscape artist should study and master the principles of arrangement, and then use his own thoughts to beautify the objects sought to be decorated.

In considering general outlines, there are certain forms of arrangement which it will prove advantageous to keep habitually in mind. Some of these might be summed up under the following heads :— GENERAL EFFECTS, RECESSES, GROUPING, PROMONTORIES, AVENUES (Natural), EXTENTS, EXPANDS, INTERMEDIATE SCENES, LEADING OBJECTS, ARTIFICIAL WORK, BOWERS, RESTS, and the like. Many of these have been already commented upon, in a more or less detailed manner.

GENERAL EFFECTS.—In the arrangements upon which our general effects are based, numerous prominent features will be found to subsist, which should always prove to be in harmony with each other, when looked at from situations which command extensive views—such as scenes looked up to from low ground, or those looked down upon from high ground. A low centre is the principle of low ground, and a high centre is the principle of high ground; the surroundings and long extents govern general effects.

RECESSES (Particular).—These should be made distinct from each other, and their number must depend on the size of the ground. They are commonly named Flower Garden, Rosetum, Rockery, Wilderness, &c. See PLATE 7 of Recesses with a regular character.

GROUPING.—This has much to do with the centres of our combinations of large or small vegetation, or water, since in this way vistas may be produced, distant scenery strengthened, lights and shades in vegetation more fully harmonized with the landscape, and the boundaries more perfectly united to the centres of scenes. See Figure 3 in PLATE 3, page 40.

PROMONTORIES.—These are of value, as imparting and keeping character true. Besides having special effects of their own, they unite various distinct outlines and yield a wider scope for our operation. Promontories serve to assist in harmonizing scenery, both aiding the grouping, the boundaries, and the general effects.

NATURAL AVENUES.—In Nature, one of the finer features of infinite beauty is made by the two higher lines of sight—that is, when a long distance is kept clear of high growing vegetation, thereby making the general outlines somewhat parallel. Shrubs and trees are capable of producing far greater effects than anything I have yet seen. Curving walks going among or through these, always give enough variety for the feelings, yet never tiring the mind, giving place to the right hand or the left, for the succession of effects. See PLATE 4.

EXPANDS.—These give great effects to the mind. See the Line of Massing, Figure 4, PLATE 3. Their qualities are particularly directed for showing effects out of the boundaries of the more perfectly kept grounds. Water scenery, in such cases, makes the most proper fences and foregrounds.

EXTENTS.—These compose a part of every scene, from miniature small vistas among the flowers and shrubs, unto extents stretching into infinity for miles away from the foreground, being curving in the form of the letter V. See Lines of Extent, Figures 3 and 4, PLATE 3, page 40.

INTERMEDIATE SCENERY.—The object of this is, with the aid of carpeting plants, shrubs, and the like, to impart a pleasing diversity to comparatively small pieces of ground, and to break the monotonous outlines of tree masses, whose chief object is to fill the proper succession of the feelings.

LEADING OBJECTS.—Each beautiful combination witnessed in decorative gardening is derived from a vast multitude of details, just as countless numbers of tiny leaves go to make up the lustrous foliage that clothes the lofty tree. In these details, however, some one object, or objects, will, by the harmonising influence which they exert as it were, challenge our especial attention.

BOWERS.—These form a somewhat important element; we may, keeping them in view, very advantageously construct our walks under graceful and fragrant climbers, or beneath trees such as the *Pinus austriaca* and others. In the latter case, the conical outlines and spiral summits yield a pleasant rich impressive onlook. Dwarf growing trees, speaking of bower effects, such as the *Ornus europæa* or Flowering Ash, often display foliage of a very agreeable character. The *Robinia Pseud-Acacia* has a most delicate leafage. The *Betula alba pendula*, or Weeping Birch, will form a light and charming bower as already said. There is, in truth, an amazing variety in respect of pleasing decorative detail. In other respects, good results will often ensue when walks are conducted through extended groups of vegetable forms, beneath dense masses of foliage.

RESTS.—Decorations included under this term are to a certain extent necessary in scenery, imparting as it were a sense of quietude and repose ; for this purpose Ivies, Vinca, Evergreen Shrubs, and the like, will answer well; nor, indeed, is there any need for much diversity. Perhaps the glades of green grass will be best understood to give rest after very extensive scenes of beauty.

When the general outlines have been decided on, according to the natural requirements of the ground, the next best thing will be to choose what are to be the most prominent features of the landscape. Tree effects will first demand consideration, then the lines of sight which shrubs and carpeting plants, respectively, are intended to occupy. In our arrangements water holds an important place, both on account of its beauty and the uses it subserves, the drainage of the land. It will frequently supply us with earth, derived from excavations, wherewith to create pleasing undulations of the surface, when this is otherwise held desirable. Nature, as is well known, produces some of her most witching effects with the aid of water. In peaceful moments, water displays, as in a magic mirror, the world around, the delicate flowers, the stately trees, rocks, the tender grass blades, nay, the scenic skies themselves, which thus seem to have a twofold existence in the depths below. The stream in its profounder course flows smoothly enough along, but in the shallows it leaps and bounds on its way with many a pleasant and fairylike cascade. The aspect of water varies much according to the distance from which it is viewed. Occasionally, indeed, when seen from afar off, and as illumined by the sun, it is eminently beautiful. Water, in truth, so numerous and varied are the combinations that we may produce with it, might well be termed a fountain of life to scenery. Therefore, the outlines of water should be as diversified as circumstance will allow. See PLATE 7, page 58.

In Nature we frequently find low lying levels occupied by water, which may often be turned to most valuable account both in natural and artificial scenery. We may thus beautify our high ground, while an excellent and efficient system of drainage may be secured ; and it will prove further desirable to have the water level some eighteen inches below the general surface. Where the view of the water is uninterrupted, the land may be lowered to the water's edge, so as not unduly to interfere with the lines of sight. As beforesaid, water is extremely well suited as a centre of scenery ; it is indeed the very life of valleys, and just as trees impart a living beauty to the outlines of hills, so does water yield harmony to the far-reaching expanses below.

In arranging the earth removed in the course of our operations, a proper gradation must be given to the surrounding curvatures of the ground. As regards the grouping of vegetable outlines and the like, the soil may often be raised so as to add to their effect and promote the general harmony of the whole. Raised ground, possessing an irregular surface, can be made to retain the principal part of the water which falls, by constructing hollows here and there on the sides in unequal step-like forms. These may frequently be seen in Nature on the declivities of hills and mountains; they tend to keep the soil beneath in a genial state of moisture at all seasons, the water filtrating gently and gradually through the masses of earth.

In imparting undulation to the surface, or in aiding undulations already formed, the general character of the soil must be kept in view. Nature, even in her irregularities, preserves a true balance and proportion, and it will not answer if we permit mere smoothness and levelness to interfere with her principles; to do this, indeed, would be to mar effects, to induce sameness instead of diversity, confusion instead of order and beauty. Ground, in truth, is often so cut up by levelling that many natural beauties entirely vanish, and the soil becomes so deteriorated by the removal of the surface that only a few of the most vigorous growing plants are able to hold up their heads. Indeed, the result is so inharmonious, that the arranger himself, seeing that something is wrong, tries to remedy the deficiency by packing plants into mere heaps; or, if money for this be forthcoming, soil is brought from a distance and piled up as a substitute for the natural diversity. But the removal of soil from any distance should only be attempted in exceptional cases; the ground itself should be laid out, and more with a view to create a comparison with the ground undulations than to produce any striking effect of contrast. Water, combined with vegetation, gives great pleasure; for, as Ruskin observes, "Eddy by eddy, the clear green streams wind along their well known beds; and, under the dark quietness of the undisturbed pines, there spring up year by year such company of joyful flowers as I know not the like of among all the blessings of the earth. It was spring time, too; and all were coming forth in clusters crowded for very love; there was room enough for all, but they crushed their leaves into all manner of strange shapes only to be nearer each other. There was the Wood Anemone, star after star, closing every now and then into nebulæ; and there was the Oxalis, troop by troop, like virginal processions of the Mois of Marie, the dark vertical clefts in the limestone choked up with them as with heavy snow, and touched with Ivy on the edges—Ivy as light and lovely as the Vine ; and ever an anon a blue gush of Violets and Cowslip bells in sunny places, and in the more open ground the Vetch, and Comfrey, and Mezereon, and the small sapphire buds of the Polygala alpina, and the Wild Strawberry, just a blossom or two all showered amidst the golden softness of deep, warm, amber-coloured moss. I came out presently on the edge of the ravine ; the solemn murmur of its waters rose suddenly from beneath, mixed with the singing of the thrushes among the Pine boughs ; and, on the opposite side of the valley, walled all along as it was by grey cliffs of limestone, there was a hawk sailing slowly off their brow, touching them nearly with his wings, and with the shadows of the Pines flickering upon his plumage from above ; but with a fall of a hundred fathoms under his breast, and the curling pools of the green river gliding and glittering dizzily beneath him, their foam globes moving with him as he flew."

The beauties of Nature prove a never-failing source of gladness. The more we see and appreciate them, the greater indeed becomes our capacity for seeing and appreciating. In respect of garden decoration, we hear it sometimes said—let this tree or that height be cleared away, so that we may get a view of the scenery beyond. This, no doubt, in some cases is right enough ; nevertheless, this cutting-down system is not one to be carried into practice without the exercise of every caution. It will not always prove well to turn two scenes into one, rather we should endeavour to make each beautiful in its way, and true in principle as in detail. With the aid of vistas, we may often greatly extend effects without destroying any scenes The indiscriminate opening-up and clearing-away system, frequently most materially detracts from the charms of a landscape, produces, in fact, a sort of bareness which is void of interest and wearisome to behold. The attempts which are sometimes made in small pleasure grounds to simulate park scenery are really quite out of place, and generally prove ridiculous failures.

No matter, indeed, how limited in extent our grounds may prove, we can always render them interesting—nay, beautiful—if we will, by the strict observance of those laws of harmonious arrangement which apply alike to the far-reaching park as to the emerald slopes of some garden fair. No attempts should ever be made so to dispose of scenery as to render it pleasing at a glance only; to do so is to cause it to pall on the attention of the observer. In other respects, although from varying points the view will of course differ, still the effects as seen from a distance should on nearer approach be always pleasing, and fulfil the expectations which the mind has formed.

In all scenery, especially in shrubberies and gardens, the different lines of sight must be duly studied. Proper attention to these will always ensure arrangements true to Nature, and effective throughout the year. It is, indeed, quite possible to attempt too much in gardens, and yet, as a general rule, the very opposite is too commonly the case, money and labour being too often expended to produce results for one year only; whereas, hardy plants once fairly established will scarcely need much more care and attention than the grass lawn which is sometimes made with a view to saving labour. Many carpeting plants, even, will cover the ground for many years, holding their own bravely against such weeds as appear, as may be witnessed in old neglected flower borders. There is a prevalent notion that a scene arranged for some one particular period can only be effective at that period. We have but to look at Nature, however, to find out our mistake, for in her domains, from the time the green leaves show themselves till they gently pass away, from the season of the sunny springtide flowers to that of the glowing fruits, there is something ever new and ever beautiful to be witnessed; and by duly following Nature's footsteps we may compass, at least approximately, some pleasing effect or other at every period of the entire year.

In what are termed technical flower gardens, the lines, whether straight or curved, should all exhibit a due proportion. Care must be taken to guard our plants from the prevailing cold winds. By proper arrangements, however, we may readily accomplish this. It often happens that a want of beauty in decorative grounds is owing, in the first instance, to faulty construction as well as to the absence of adequate attention during the earlier stages of plant growth.

In respect of general arrangements, whether it be a question of a nobleman's estate, or a villa in the vicinity of some large town, they are often carried out in quite too hasty a fashion. Frequently, the plan for a town park will be selected, not on account of its intrinsic merits for laying out soil to best advantage, but rather for some quite secondary motive—for instance, a show of colour, or some knack of design in the execution. Many a fair plot of soil has thus been spoiled, when even a slight acquaintance with the laws of scenery, in principle and detail, might have led to very different results.

Experience, doubtless, is a great school—its lessons all may learn. Still, it is scarcely fair to the land, when a person who has perhaps been engaged during his whole previous life in occupations having no connexion with landscape scenery, begins off-hand to decorate and, perhaps after a long period of failure and blundering, learns too late what loveliness once was, but is now no longer possible.

At other times, much injury arises from the mistakes of men possibly conversant with some particular branch, but ignorant of the general principles of laying out land, and who therefore "cut up the ground." Persons such as these will often attach themselves to the cultivation of particular plants to the exclusion of others; or haply fancy the construction and embellishment of walks to be the important all-in-all; or some other matters of detail, well in their own place, but which have no right to take the place of scenery, so as to preponderate.

The first thing necessary in plan making is to have a basis to work upon. The heights and hollows should be pricked on paper, the water courses, quality of soil, prevalent winds, and objects to be concealed all set down. This will enable the mind to grasp the entire arrangement, and yield the very greatest assistance in properly apportioning our landscapes.

In giving the list of the principal diversifications of scenery, I venture to recapitulate or sum together a few of the remarks already made for arrangement.

The land is not level or straight, but is full of recesses, promontories, surfaces going into heights or hollows, and vegetation itself has an infinity of forms; therefore, the general principle of Nature is undulation, which is composed of curvature, the line of Nature ever and anon curving to you or from you. In PLATE No. 3 these lines are shown harshly for the sake of illustration, the line of mass coming to you and the lines of extents going from you. If these two lines are watched closely in Nature's land and vegetation they will give the Present and Future, thus coinciding with the very thoughts of our existence, and feeding the wants of the mind suitable to its life. The Present line is where the line curves to you, and the Future line is where the line curves from you. From a just arrangement of these lines, according to the curvature of the character in course of arrangement, the line of beauty should come in the general effect, aiming at clearness in the Present line to infinity in the Future.

In speaking of colour in general terms, I may say that the subject must be learnt from Nature more than from books.

Strong colours are like the voice of Nature speaking to mankind in tones that all can hear; but she does more than this: she feeds the most delicate minds that love her as if to tell them her thoughts; she shows infinite colours according to their feelings as possessed by each person who lives in a world of his own. These colours are sometimes acknowledged as tints, lights, and shades of vegetation, meaning a great deal to some, and nothing at all to others.

The arrangement of colour should be guided by the impressions produced upon the mind. Good impressions may be divided into light and impressive thoughts, the mind acquiring complete satisfaction by the succession of various feelings going from one to the other. Thoughts are light or impressive, according to their quality—for example, to take the two extremes, light thoughts give temporary pleasure, and impressive thoughts do more—they give satisfaction.

All colour perhaps might be called light, dark, or medium, in very general terms, so as to form a principle or guide for the development of the characters in course of arrangement.

In beauty, form and colour are one; its form giving you Nature's character for the present and future; while its colour tells you its permanent impressions or its light joyous present thoughts.

The material from out of which beauty is to be evolved must always be worked up with an object before effects can be realised; therefore, first seek out the object to be gained. Each separate object, from the greatest general effect to the smallest detail, expresses a principle in itself. There is no equality in Nature, as Nature forms her plants of different parts, leaves, &c. The small hills assist the larger hills, and these assist the mountains in mountainous country, showing an activity serving some particular principle in beauty which may be called power. The principle she builds her beauties upon is comparison, the different parts assisting each other's beauty, and these in proportional parts in union to each other, balancing together to produce harmony.

Beauty is the food for the stimulation of feelings nobly to satisfaction for feeding the mind with good thoughts.

The first use of the knowledge gained respecting beauty will be to arrange the various particulars into order. You begin by selecting the sites which afford the greater variety of scenery the proportions of the ground can give; and then form the principal outlines, such as long distances, recesses, promontories, and groups, in accordance with the natural undulation and other circumstances of the domain, the effects of the boundaries, or whatever other wants may be apparent. Thus when the general outlines are decided upon, the characters of vegetation may be chosen to clothe the earth according to the directions already given, being true to the curvature of each character and uniting the general whole in harmony. One principle to be observed in producing harmony, is, that each of the three lines of sight must receive its just proportion of effects in accordance with the circumstances of the character developed, so that at whatever distance the sites are placed, the whole of the land effects will be observed to make the scene complete.

The lines of distances are not the placing of the subjects to be seen from some particular site only, but to enable you to receive satisfaction from every distance at which it is possible to view the scene. For instance, in looking at some particular view of vegetation, you see the details, leaves, flowers, &c., in the foreground; move into the middistance and you see these details forming combinations with each other, producing masses which assist the larger forms of vegetation; while in the distance you see the general outlines or objects gained, and, although you cannot see the details on the tops of the trees, still they are there combining into the forms which you can see. Thus in properly arranged scenery it is impossible for the lines of distance to be in any case wrong.

When the parts belonging to scenery are learned, they will be found to constitute two divisions—viz., *The Scene and its Outlines.*

SCENERY—PRINCIPLES.

This division, which is in reality imaginary, may be observed in all scenery from that of the most extended character to the very smallest effects. By the development of this principle, according to the principles of Nature, man may give perpetual beauty to his arrangements.

In beautifying land there are two great divisions of the year observed, which may in a broad way be termed winter and summer. These two contain within themselves a vast number of effects, but these wants can be fully provided for by the principles spoken of in the last paragraph—The Scene and its Outlines. The winter effects are principally produced in the outlines, and the summer effects in the scene, producing a succession of special beauties blending harmoniously together, so that each during its period is complete of itself, and afterwards assists the general character of the scenery.

Each effect of scenery has its own particular beauty, its distinctive quality from any other, but notwithstanding this there are twelve general forms so distinctive that we venture to call them principal effects for assisting the mind in giving general successional feelings to scenery.

Style is the arrangement of scenery for supplying some particular *general* want to the feelings of mankind. To this subject we now turn.

PRINCIPAL DIVERSIFICATIONS OF SCENERY.

Material { Land. Water. Vegetation. } Diversifications of Scenery. { Beauty (Book I.) Laws of Order (Book II.) Principal Effects and Styles of Scenery (Book III.) }

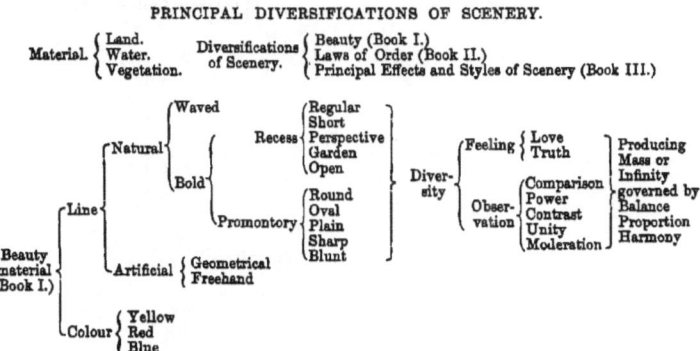

PRINCIPAL DIVERSIFICATIONS OF SCENERY—*(Continued).*

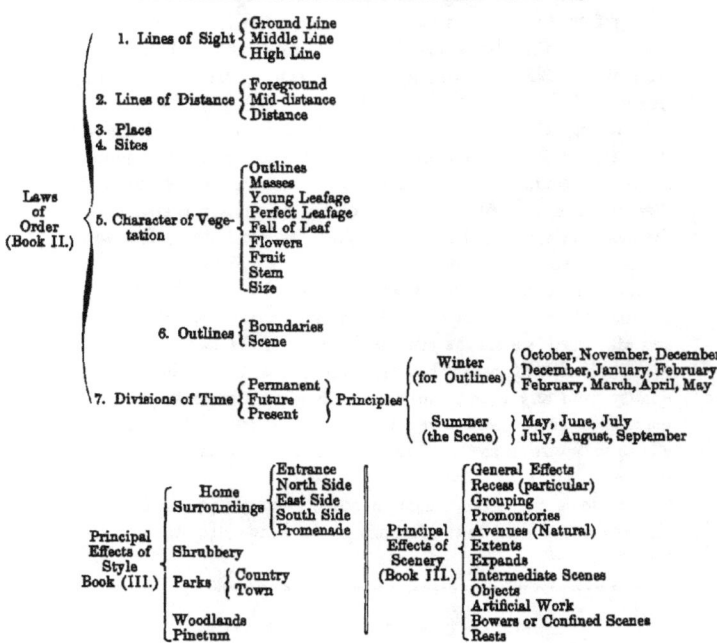

CHAPTER II.

STYLE.

To beautify land with success, it will be needful not only to put thought, but love also into our work. It will be requisite, not merely to be familiar with the names of the plants with which we are to deal, but, likewise, with their individual characteristics, and with the various circumstances and combinations in which they may be placed.

There are two well marked divisions in scenery—namely, those which are distinguished by natural, and those by artificial effects. Artificial scenery is properly contiguous to buildings, with whose outlines it will best harmonize ; while natural scenery will prove most compatible with our efforts to beautify the land in various uses. The various styles of scenery may be thus classed :—

$$\text{Styles} \begin{cases} \text{Home Scenery} \\ \text{Shrubbery} \\ \text{Parks} \begin{cases} \text{Natural} \\ \text{Artificial} \end{cases} \\ \text{Woodlands} \\ \text{Pinetum} \end{cases}$$

In Home Scenery, we may have technical refinement assisting Nature ; in Shrubberies, the natural refining principles of the lower lines of sight ; in Parks and Pinetum, the natural refinement; each having its particular principle ; and Woodlands show Nature in her wild effects. Each style produces its own particular impression, and gives rise to its own especial gratification.

HOME SCENERY.

Ground, in the immediate neighbourhood of residences, as well as buildings appertaining to these, requires a particular adjustment, not only that it may subserve all necessary purposes, but likewise that it may yield its fitting quota of embellishment to the general scene. It must first be our study to make our decorations harmonize with the outlines of the mansion, and then with each part of it as viewed in detail. Our efforts in this way will at first be in the direction of surfaces straight and curved—formal outlines, and strong colours; these gradually blending, by means of intermediate forms and hues, with the natural undulations; so that whether we view the landscape from the window, or sallying out, survey the house and its surroundings, the impression on the mind will be soothing and agreeable, though in different degrees. Houses, as a general rule, are built too much alike, but we may always contrive that their environments shall exhibit each its own special arrangement, in harmony with the surrounding landscape. Home Scenery, so to speak, has rarely full justice done it. The ground near a house may be right, but the natural outlines beyond will often be either forgotten, or else permitted to assume an almost wild aspect, in contiguity to the formal garden and mansion itself. Instead of which, the edifice should form a jewel of which the scenery in the immediate surrounding is the setting; in short, a portrait to which it is as the drapery. We abandon the bleak summit to obtain shelter from the cutting winds, inimical alike to animal and vegetable life; and, therefore, calculated to deprive such a position of those appropriate and ornamental accompaniments, which are so essential to a perfect dwelling. The depression of the valley must also be avoided, on account of dampness, stagnant air, want of prospect, and further, because a house is never seen to greater disadvantage than when it is looked down upon. Some elevated knoll or slope, high enough to command the distant view, yet not too high for easy approach, backed by Woodland, and surrounded within easy distance by foliage, will afford the greatest combination of natural advantages to each side; and a house so seated will form an agreeable object when looked upon from a distance, as it neither falls below the horizon, nor rudely breaks the sky-line. The various items that go to make up a home scene, will depend very much on circumstances. The sunlight is fraught with such numberless advantages, that an abundant supply of it will prove one of our very best coadjutors. For this reason, the north side of a residence must hold a lower place in our regard than the south. Trees of the Fir tribe afford excellent shelter where it proves desirable, in many cases they may be arranged so as to protect both sides of a dwelling, and soften the northern and north-eastern blasts. Fir Trees look well when disposed in curves, sufficiently far off, however, to display to advantage their varying lights and shades, as well as to prevent them from in any wise intercepting the sunshine. Evergreens, in general, give as it were stability to scenery, and take an important share in decorations in the vicinity of mansions.

In our endeavours to assimilate distant views and expanses with those more immediately contiguous to the dwelling-house it will often prove of excellent service. To use plants that may occupy an intermediate position, so to speak, between the artistic portion of the landscape and the natural undulations beyond, as well as to have something in common with both. For example, the *Juniperus communis hibernica,* by its columnar character of growth, will be quite in keeping with the formal outlines of the middle line of sight belonging to a mansion, while its silvery hues will well harmonise with specimens of the *Pinus excelsa* at a greater distance. In home scenery—as indeed in all other—the lines of sight must receive due consideration. A tree or two may, as it were, break away from the more general masses, so as to impart quantity and shade, and increase the diversity. As respects carpeting plants and shrubs, these should receive full development in our foreground. Shrubs, indeed, when properly handled, produce very successful results nigh a dwelling. As they do not rise above twenty feet, they can thus be brought nearer than many trees, and by their cheerful forms and colours serve to brighten the scene.

Each of our plants should display a certain fitness and harmony with its surroundings. There should, if I may so express myself, be no merely heaped-up vegetation. When possible, each beautiful feature a plant may happen to possess should be displayed with loving care. It requires, no doubt, considerable space to do full justice to the various characters of vegetable growths, still we have parks, demesnes, public gardens, and the like in abundance, where the more hardy species may have ample room allotted to them. Notwithstanding this, in many a pleasure ground laid out by some merchant prince or other, where there is a wide tract of soil and, it might be presumed, shelter and care for every plant that grew, there is hardly an equivalent return for the money that has been expended. The owner, very probably, has had the ground arranged according to his own ideas, and finds, when too late, his mistake. In fact, as much thought, and experience, and care, are requisite to arrange land according to the laws of beauty and usefulness, as are needed to amass a fortune. We find, perhaps, in such cases, a few parallel borders of trees and shrubs so thickly planted that scarcely a single real feature of one of them is discernible. Far more care, in truth, is shown in planting a hedge of trees around the boundary of the ground, so that its extent may be apparent, than in bringing into view the beauty of the scenery around. Probably, near the grounds intended to be ornamental and facing the trees, we shall see a one-sided hedge—for no other term so well expresses its appearance—composed of evergreen shrubs, each shrub showing about one-third of its surface. Then next the foreground plants are dotted about, with here and there perhaps some among them quite new and fashionable—all, as it were, standing witnesses against the harsh treatment which they receive. Such results as these, unfortunately, can be seen in a multitude of instances in different parts of our islands, never, in fact, productive of any of the real or true characters of vegetation. Plants are removed and replanted in the vain hope that they will do well—a result which is seldom achieved.

The boundaries of our home scenery, aided by suitable growths, may, with great propriety, be made to assume much of the irregularity of natural outlines, every advantage being taken of any recesses that may subsist. Vegetation, in newly-planted places, will require attention as it progresses, growths used for present effects requiring to be removed as others more permanent, attain development. If a plot of ground be properly laid out, it will be impossible for the owner, if he be a person of any good taste, ever to become tired of it; for here, indeed, each year would add a fresh beauty and develop its character, unseen before, and the pleasure of arranging them is great. For, as Repton so well remarks: "The most valuable lesson now left me to communicate is this—I am convinced that the delight I have always taken in landscapes and gardens, without any reference to their quantity or appropriation, or without caring whether they are forests or rosaries, or whether they were palaces, villas, or cottages, while I had leave to admire their beauties and even to direct their improvement, has been the chief source of that large portion of happiness which I have enjoyed through life."

Residences of the villa order will not need so many formal adjustments as do structures of greater pretensions, and will thus, and with a lesser expenditure, more readily assimilate themselves to Nature's outlines. However limited in extent may be the land we have to deal with, there should always be a clear, well-defined foreground and back-ground, together with a natural blending of effects, according to its character, but not so as to convey a confused impression. Let all characters be clear, departing into infinity of the boundaries, giving true character to satisfaction.

Every arrangement should, if possible, display some variety of feature. When, indeed, the place is small, we may lessen larger subjects, and so arrange trees as to assist the effects of shrubs, and thus prevent them from injuring the smaller growths beneath them. "Dimensions, whether large or small, have but slight influence on the merit of a design. Fitness and beauty are almost independent of size, just as a miniature may be more excellent than a kit-cat."* There should be no attempt in a villa garden to imitate that of a palace, and, generally speaking, in villa effects the house should, so to say, be subservient to Nature, and not contrariwise. In arranging the surroundings of a residence, it would be unreasonable to suppose that the front entrance or back offices, or even the flower-garden should occupy nearly all the ground about the place. Yet often it happens that an undue proportion of surface is taken up with one or other of these. Instead of this, each feature should receive a fitting attention and development commensurate with its importance.

We may here enumerate the four sides of a residence as follows:

Entrance,	West Front.
Offices,	North.
Home Scene,	East.
Grand Scene,	South.

WEST FRONT.
The Entrance.

The entrance to a residence will vary, of course, according to its character. Magnificent approaches, flanked by noble trees, beseem our palaces, whose iron gates glitter with gilding, and whose walls and

* Morris: "A House for the Suburb."

turrets as we approach combine in one picture with many a noble specimen of vegetation ; while in the sunny glades on either side lie basking the graceful deer. But other entrances than such as these abound, not, perhaps, so striking, but probably equally beautiful, it matters not how humble the dwelling, if only its natural advantages be made the most of, the approach to it will yield us pleasure. As respects the arrangement of vegetable growths for an entrance, the trees might be arranged so as to yield glimpses of the scenery beyond. Care, however, must be taken to preserve the best scenery for the chief effects ; therefore an entrance must not occupy too prominent a position in respect of decoration.

As much protection as possible should be afforded from cold winds by means of undulating ground, trees, and the like. The site of building, say a little to the east or to the west, will often yield protection from cold, and yet not unduly diminish the sun's light. A western entrance commands a view of the setting sun gilding the landscape ere his rays finally disappear. Much of the vegetation employed for entrances might be of a deciduous character, so as to tell the season. Evergreen growths, however, should subsist in sufficient abundance to produce permanent effects. Trees commonly answer our purposes best, but shrubs enough must also be employed, so as to enliven the middle line of sight, and act as mediums between the undulating ground-surface and the tree effects. The variety of plants made use of, as also the disposal of these, will depend much on circumstances. Should striking colour be required, gold will admirably light up an entrance scene. At the same time, the natural outlines of the different growths should as much as possible be preserved. Occasionally, the drives leading through a park, may be made to disclose, here and there, the most lovely vistas. Still the drives themselves are not *per se* a decorative beauty, and the tasteless corkscrew curves, sometimes imparted to them when approaching some small place or other, serve no ornamental purpose whatever. The drive is subordinate to the house, and is not intended to show off its own beauty merely, or display the owner's possessions. It may, however, assist in decoration, by a suitable curvature in the direction of the dwelling.

As regards planting near a house, private walks to serve as a promenade, may often be made to turn out to much advantage. If possible, they should have a sunny exposure, and be so arranged as to furnish, unobserved, notice of the approach of visitors. Otherwise, such walks comport admirably with woodland scenery. Evergreen plants, here and there, yield verdant recesses the winter through. On dry slopes there might be masses of sweet-scented plants, while in retired nooks the *Populus tremula* might whisper its secrets to the summer winds.

SOUTH FRONT.

Home Scenery—The Flower Garden.

The south front ought to be held private, since it is here that we shall best develop the hidden beauty of the situation and decorate our buildings withal. Here, too, the sun will afford us the greatest assistance, and things, in general, will assume more of a festive character, by reason of their being remote from the public entrance leading to the mansion and offices. It is at this side also that the drawing-room should be placed.

It would, indeed, be altogether difficult to estimate the amount of thought, care, and skill that have in different ages been expended on gardens and flowers. In the infancy of society, separate vegetable, fruit, and flower gardens, most probably did not subsist. But as mankind advanced in civilisation and refinement, the number of plants to be cultivated increased, so that it became needful to create distinct departments for them. In all ages, flowers have been a joy and a delight. From the earliest times, poets have sung their glories. In Shakspeare, the love of their sweet graces is so conspicuous that it has led to the surmise that at some period or other he might have been engaged in gardening as a pastime, if not a profession. Formal symmetrical arrangements held at one time great sway. The Italian garden, to a considerable extent, was, as it were, an expansion of the buildings which it surrounded. No device, however, that ever yet the heart of man conceived, can hope entirely to rival the inimitable charm which can be accomplished by assisting Nature. Formal arrangements, indeed, are costly to produce and to keep in order, but those of Nature are ever within our reach. Shakspeare himself speaks of "natural graces that extinguish art." These formal gardens are, as it were, floral margins to palaces, with outlines and designs abounding in living structures sweet and fair, lighting up the scene with their brilliant beauty, and marking the transition between the natural and the artificial.

When we have duly studied the intent and meaning of the house, we shall have a base to work upon as regards the drawing up of a design for the garden. This, if possible, should always lie sloping to the south. If it be a case in which statues, vases, fountains, and the like, prove desirable, these might be made as if to supply some want, or fulfil some purpose, avoiding at the same time all confusion. The bedding-out system yields material for a display to which Herbaceous plants alone are commonly not equal. Many vegetable growths, such as Pelargoniums and the blue Lobelia, will render the outlook gay from June till October. Herbaceous plants, useful as thus, are greatly appreciated by gardeners, inasmuch as they call for but little attention when once well established. There are also many varieties of hardy plants, not generally known, that might be turned to very extensive account in gardens. Some of these, indeed, would even contribute to permanent effects, and produce in the end very valuable results. Houses built on high ground often render a terraced arrangement desirable. There may be, as thus, in connection with the mansion an architectural succession of terraces. Of these, the first might include the flower garden, whose outlines, while they lent themselves somewhat to the formal contours of the building, should also lean towards Nature's gentle curves. The next terrace, marking, as it were, the boundary line between Art and Nature, might be characterised by grassy slopes and banks of suitable form and outline, sufficiently adapted to the growth of whatever form of vegetation it might be deemed most expedient to plant thereon. The occasions are few in which unproductive grass banks shall be needed, which else are apt to prove an injury rather than a benefit; these should have various forms of plant life in an outline of curvature according to the character required. Some details may be borrowed from the higher terraces, and thus contribute to the harmony of the whole. It must, however, be noted that growths of a loftier stature than that of carpeting plants must prove the distinguishing feature of connecting the terraces together, as this is one of the chief faults of the present arrangement.

Should there be no need for terraces very lovely effects can be developed on hilly ground by following in Nature's footsteps. Where the incline, however, is rapid, terraces, when introduced, may be diversified by minor ones, each stamped by some particular feature affording a pleasure all its own. We must ever bear in mind, however, that no mere technical display is called for, but simply the fitting arrangement of lovely flowers, combining with buildings and light forms of vegetation. Terrace flower beds may occupy the general level, or be raised above it, or sunk beneath it, as circumstances may require. The character of your form (curvature) is that only to which you are bound to be true.

Trees must be few in the boundaries in proximity to the front of a mansion. Assistance, however, can be gained from a proper use of the middle line of subjects (shrubs), and in these lines of sight climbers can give considerable aid, as they do not interfere with any ground effects. Their gracefulness and perfume give warmth and assist in taking away the coldness of these formal gardens. These plants can be arranged to any inflexion wanted for the garden curvature. The beauty of climbing and creeping plants is often seriously marred by the arrangement used for their display; material, such as light wire work, suitable enough for the cage of some feathered songster, but hardly adapted to support a plant throughout a number of years, being employed for this purpose. Often, the low price at which this wire work may be had, constitutes an inducement, a very insufficient one, however, to purchase it. We see it twisted about in every variety of form and fashion, but without any adequate regard to the growth of the plants which it assumes to support; the result of which is that it gives way at the first imperious blast of wind. Climbing plants, in all their rich and various beauty, are, indeed, a source of the utmost enjoyment. It seems as though in them Nature vied with man in decorating his dwelling and enhancing the work of his hands. Whether we view them as twining round the cottage portal, or hanging in exquisite festoons from some terraced balustrade, they are ever graceful and lovely. Many a spot, otherwise uninteresting, do they render bright and cheerful. We have the Climbing Rose and the Honeysuckle, the Clematis, purple, white, and blue, the Jasmine, and a number of others, at once fragrant and gay, which, whether they cluster round our windows, or combine to form the pretty tracery on the rustic baskets in our grounds, are alike a joy and a delight.

In towns, too frequently, the merits of climbing plants meet with but sparse recognition; and yet, when judiciously resorted to, they constitute a most important element of cheerfulness, shed, indeed, a perfect grace on otherwise the barest surroundings. Ivy, so commonly chosen for covering walls, can have its own place and still leave room for other plants. Many forms possess a wealth of foliage and flowers in due season that adapt them admirably for this purpose. We have also the sunny Vine, Virginian Creeper, with others, right well suited for wall and trellis decoration. At first, indeed, they would need some little attention, but as our climbers grow in stature they most amply repay any trouble which they may have occasioned. In the west end of London most graceful effects are produced by the careful training of the Virginian Creeper and some of the hardy kinds of Ivy on the walls of private residences. A verandah or other ornamental outline, well covered with climbers, will often look very gay on an otherwise dead wall. Pillars intended to be covered with creepers must have bases of a proportion suited to the weight which they will have to bear. In the matter of festooning and arching, there ought to be as much diversity as possible. Climbers for promenades should be arranged in bold sweeping curves, or, if meant to be viewed from a distance, should project here and there. Much money is spent sometimes upon artistic embellishments for gardens of questionable character, but structures for climbers might be made suitable for many characters of scenery.

As respects flower-beds, decorations out of all proportion and character in the mid-line of sight are only too often attempted, such, for example, as sticking the Irish Yew, *Taxus baccata fastigiata* or *Cupressus Lawsoniana*, which do not harmonise in the least with the other plants, in the very centre of a large round flower-bed. Instead of this such growths ought to occupy some position in unison with the design of which they form a part. To assist the middle line of sight large figures are more suitable for flower beds than small; they yield greater scope for permanent edgings as well as for the introduction of shrubs and climbers, so as to prevent an appearance of flatness and serve as connecting links with the vegetation beyond, as well as assisting the general diversification.

Gardens, as a general rule, should be lowest in the centre. The outlines of designs ought to be defined by permanent veiling plants, which may assist our summer effects by their various light and shade. Growths of this kind often put forth their blooms in early spring. They should not prove mere narrow stripes but occupy a due proportion in form and size to the flower-beds or borders, and while they set off, other combinations might display a character and beauty of their own. Of hardy edging, much of which consists of alpine plants, we possess an immense variety. Some of these suit shady, others sunny situations; some are adapted for dry places, others for moist. They supply a want much felt in respect of permanent decoration. Many of them, however, will not answer with water in close juxtaposition, and in such case it will be well to raise the ground somewhat round the edging. This being done they will grow and flourish, displaying beauties far surpassing those of any stone work that might be devised. The *Sedum*, along with various kinds of *Saxifraga* and *Sempervivum*, forms capital edgings. I have made many of these edgings with excellent results. *Sedum acre aureum* forms perfect cushions of gold from the beginning of March till the end of May. Its foliage is lighter in tint than that of the grass, and is occasionally very useful in summer effects; and from the midst of these edgings should spring hosts of flowers from bulbous plants. The permanent plants, shrubs, and edgings, should assist to give effects at dormant periods of the year, and thus keep a complete succession by being arranged into an effect suitable either for themselves or combining with other plants.

In respect of flower-beds, the most brilliant colours should occupy a position rather towards the boundaries than the centres. As regards bedding-out, much care is required to ascertain the plants that suit the various distances from the eye; especially in large beds should each subject have suitable distances. Certain varieties of *Pelargonium*, which, when near at hand, look very beautiful, quite lose their effect when viewed from afar. It is usual to have, as it were, a master colour in each scene. Blue, perhaps, will yield us the best effects of any; but let us have as many permanent combinations as possible, to enliven our gardens when the flowers of spring and summer are absent.

Thus we may always have something cheerful to greet the eye from the; me the Aconite shines out in January, till the period of the Christmas Rose. Springtime and summer are the gala times of these special effects of flower-gardens, when they will exhibit all their rich and various array, if properly arranged and established.

Wordsworth seemed to have appreciated the spirit of the scenery suitable to the south front of a palace, when writing the following lines:—

> "A single step has freed me from the skirts
> Of the blind vapour, opened to my view,
> Glory beyond all glory ever seen
> By waking sense or by the dreaming soul.
> The appearance, instantaneously disclosed,
> Was of a mighty city—boldly say
> A wilderness of buildings—sinking far,
> And self-withdrawn into a boundless depth,
> Far sinking into splendour, without end,
> Fabric it seemed of diamond and of gold,
> With alabaster domes, and silver spires,
> And blazing terrace upon terrace, high
> Uplifted ; here, serene pavilions bright
> In avenues disposed ; there, towers begirt
> With battlements that on their restless fronts
> Bore stars—illuminations of all gems."

EAST FRONT.
(Home Scenery continued)—Reserve Garden.

Before examining the East Front it will be advantageous to make a few remarks upon the Reserve Garden as an introduction thereto.

These gardens are quite essential for the decoration of ornamental grounds, especially where our aim is the production of hardy plants. In a Reserve Garden we can have material at hand to supply any deficiency that, from unforeseen causes, may arise. We have plant houses for the production of decorative plants, so termed. The same want subsists with regard to the varieties of hardy plants. As respects their growth and development, a fair piece of land of suitable size, with good deep drainage will best answer the purpose. It should be well sheltered, but tree roots ought not to be suffered to engross the soil, and free scope should be allowed for the fostering of the more delicate growths.

The arrangement of the surface, indeed, should be adapted to the various conditions of the plants that are to occupy it. The soil ought to be of a good loamy description, and in places where it may be found desirable to make banks, the soil might be lighter. For plants such as the *Sedums*, the ground might be made into raised beds above the general level; for others, sunk beds will prove more advantageous, in order to preserve the moistness of the soil for the sake of plants —some Lilies, for example, with their fleshy succulent roots. The soil should likewise be treated with certain exceptional composts, some of these being made up of leaf mould and some of peat mould. When the sunk beds and prepared land do not furnish earth enough for our raised beds we may lower the walks and so construct them within a few hours. Judicious arrangements will yield ample facilities for the culture of the many varieties of hardy plants. Some of these, when small, as sometimes obtained from nurseries, it will be well to place for a year or two in some reserved spot before calling on them for more open display.

In Belgian nurseries it is quite common to find numerous low beds, formed of leaf-mould a foot or fifteen inches in depth, in readiness for subjects, such as *Azalea indica*, and others, meant to be planted out in the course of the summer. This mould is often in the form of autumn leaves, carted from a long distance. It serves as a capital means of protection in the first instance. Leaf-mould, in truth, seems to be Nature's nursery for young plants. Gardeners most fully appreciate its advantages, even for growths that require loam when fully established. Nursery grounds, where the soil is strong and heavy, might be greatly improved were the cart roads lowered a foot or two below their general level, so as to drain and air the soil. Of course the outfall must be properly looked to. By this means the subsoil will be benefited to a much greater extent than what might beforehand be imagined.

NATURAL GARDENING.

We have glanced at the entrance and what might be called the grand front of the residence. If the principal apartments be towards the south, the more quiet morning rooms might be judiciously situated at the east. Ground which is left a little bare at this side, kept for comparison with the building, could be used for various out-door games—bowls, for example, and croquet; not cricket however, the park being best adapted for this amusement. The east side, too, having the advantage of the morning sun, will be found pleasantest for occupation in the early part of the day. Natural arrangements rather than formal ones, will here best serve our purposes. We shall find on experience that plants require diversified situations, so that a sufficing quantity of sunlight shall fall to their share, adequate, at least, to develop all their natural loveliness. They all, indeed, stand in need of air, water, and sustenance, although not in like proportions; the supply of these important elements, severally, being vastly greater in some cases than in others. To give a plant its proper position, is, in fact, the chief object to aim at, since in this must mainly reside its life and growth. An adequate water supply is perfectly indispensable. The *Lemna*, or Duckweed, derives its sustenance from air and water only. In other cases, plants generally vary greatly as to the quantity of water which they require. The amount of moisture which some vegetable growths dispose of is really prodigious. The Sunflower and *Eucalyptus globulus*, in climates warmer than that of Great Britain, the latter particularly, are actually said to have the power of draining marshy soil, and of annihilating malarious exhalations as well. Occasionally we meet with plants that almost do without water; but there are none that can altogether subsist without air and water. This fact, however, has not met with sufficient recognition; and very often the promise of a fair yield of grapes has been rendered abortive owing to insufficient air supply from the time they begin to colour till they become ripe. As respects out-door gardening, the water supply is most important. Some plants would almost require a marsh for their development, while others again need a constant and yet graduated moisture throughout the year, without, however, being sodden. Some demand a constant humidity, but will not put up with being wet about the collar of the plants.

The food, or, more properly, the soil that plants require varies exceedingly in quality and quantity, as in depth, shallowness, lightness or otherwise, according to circumstances. Cultivators, generally, are well aware of these requirements, but do not always take the best method of meeting them. Lovers of Nature, who have studied the original habitats of vegetable growths, know how admirably the wants of these growths are there supplied. In gardens and other decorated surfaces, the soil, so far as means for doing so are forthcoming, is levelled. At the same time, and exclusive of the bedding-out system, a few plants are usually dotted about the borders. Occasionally, indeed, a large portion of the surface is intentionally left bare, and hoed, and raked nearly once a week, and this too in the summer time, when the sun does his very best to encourage the vegetable growths. Such faulty arrangements in violation of Nature's requirements, are only too common. And notwithstanding the large amount of land planted for beauty, it is quite unusual to see fine specimens of the three lines of sight blending together producing harmonious scenery.

When we consider Nature's ways, and how she supplies the incessant requirements of vegetable life, we find, in the first place, the soil almost infinitely varied, no two forms being quite alike. Low-lying grounds she clothes with one form of structures; high levels with some other. On a green hill-side, for example, even in the course of a short walk, we see numerous varieties of plants flourishing within perhaps a few yards of each other. In grounds that undulate, the heights and hollows form a natural system of drainage, giving to each structure the air, water, and soil most needed. Nature, however, reveals her secrets only to those who seek her in love—cold criticism looks in vain. She spreads her lovely carpet, and presents us with a wealth of delicate flowers ministering to our delights in countless numbers. "Being thus prepared for us in all ways, and made beautiful and good for food, and for building, and for instruments of our hands, this race of plants deserving boundless affection and admiration from us, become, in proportion to their obtaining it, a nearly perfect test of our being in right temper of mind and way of life—so that no one can be far wrong in either who loves the trees enough, and every one is assuredly wrong in both who does not love them, if his life has brought them in his way."*

Nature, so to speak, is never entirely level or perfectly straight, but abounds with such gentle and insensible gradations that, often, one has to retire to some distance in order to discern the actual curvature of the soil. In beginning to decorate, existing undulations should be rendered as effective as possible. Towards the east front of a residence a natural garden may be constructed. When properly managed, it is quite surprising how many charming results can be

* Modern Painters, vol. v.

accomplished. In fact, the more uneven the ground, the better will it be found to suit our purposes. In the case of new houses, the soil obtained in excavating foundations may often be turned to excellent account, and desirable changes may be effected at much less cost than what is commonly occasioned by levelling. The central portion, generally speaking, should preserve a sort of hollow so as not to interfere with the view. When possible, we should make the heights higher and the hollows lower, so as to harmonise with the surroundings. The walks about should be gently led over the different surfaces, yielding access to the best views, each presenting something new. Situations out of character with the scenery, may be so planted as to hinder them from impairing the outlook.

To convey an idea of the varied forms which gardens may assume is no easy matter. In fact, they vary in almost every detail. If only rightly managed, they may be made the source of the purest enjoyment. The ancients, it is said, were fond of surveying the sunny blossoms in their pleasure grounds. A writer in the "Quarterly," some years back, speaks with high encomium of the Hollyhock, which, it has been said, is almost the only landscape flower we possess. "So picturesque is it," remarks the writer alluded to, "that perhaps no artist ever attempted to draw a garden without introducing it, whether it were really there or not. By far the finest effect that combined Art and Nature ever produced in gardening were those fine masses of many coloured hollyhocks clustered round a weather-tinted vase, such as Sir Joshua delighted to place in the wings of his pictures."

Gardens, when they approach a dwelling, may assume a somewhat formal and artistic aspect; at least, the outlines of house and garden should adequately harmonise. Views and distances, as before observed, should be held in due remembrance. The outline plans will show how the surface can be best diversified. Thus rising grounds can be covered with what we may term veiling plants, but in truth there are a multitude of growths which impart the most agreeable effects, and afford scope for decoration that more formal arrangements lack. Undulating ground in itself is a great advantage, giving sheltered nooks for tender plants in one place, shady recesses in others, and spots where the greatest possible sunlight will be supplied to such growths as most require it. If only we should be fortunate enough to have some crystal spring or rivulet within the grounds, it will admirably subserve our purposes, and yield an opening for lilies and other water plants if we desire them. Climbers and creepers of various kinds impart a wild romantic aspect; and if it be in spring, we may have the glorious double-flowered Gorse, the Furze Linnæus, on first beholding, we are told, fell down and worshipped, Anemones, Primroses, Violets, and many others. If, indeed, it be in character with the surroundings, we can have resort to the Honeysuckles, the masses of odorous flowers rising from the very grass itself. We must, however, take care that the ground shall be entirely covered with vegetation in keeping with the scene. In selecting strong colours for developing the effects, it will generally be found that silver-hued plants will be found effective for the delicate lights of morning. When, however, gardens in the natural style become more sought after, further improvements will doubtless be made as regards their arrangement. In the preceding pages, I have merely given a few hints respecting the method to be pursued in home gardening and decoration, and a house of rather large dimensions may have other characters for its various sides. It will always prove desirable to have a garden entrance, and others, in proportion to the size of the mansion, as giving access, it may be, to a deer park, or merely serving as a comfortable inlet and outlet for the family away from the general entrance.

In a mansion of greater pretensions we shall look for a larger amount of decoration, but this, in every case, should be in character with the surroundings, combining at once the useful and the beautiful so far, at least, as balance, stability, and reposing satisfaction, are calculated to compass both.

"Words, phrases, fashions, all may pass away,
But Truth and Nature never shall decay."

The undulations of these gardens can take a character of curvature suitable to the house or the most natural wild scenery, thus becoming suitable to any character a natural garden is required for. The soil can be held up by numerous plants, such as are mentioned in the Hardy Plant Catalogues published of late years and which most of the gardening public will have in their possession; thus I need not give particulars of a subject which has already been done by others.

These gardens can develop the three lines of vegetation in great beauty, according to the character they exhibit.

R

CHAPTER III.

SHRUBS—STYLE.

SHRUBBERIES, so termed, possess many advantages for exhibiting the manifold beauties of the hardy forms of vegetable life. The great number of plants brought from various parts, and therein naturalised, demand for their fitting development numerous conditions of light, air, soil, and water, which can only be adequately realised in large spaces of ground where diversity of outline abounds.

Inasmuch as each specimen of plant life produces an impression proportionate to the distance from the eye at which it is situated, and according to the trees, shrubs, or carpeting plants which fill up the principal lines of sight, so in the style which we are at present considering, shrubs form the leading feature, while trees, flowers, and the like, each in their own place, will assist the general harmony.

In order that the characteristics of any particular form of vegetation may be duly evolved, it will be requisite, as already stated, that the place which it shall occupy should be one sufficiently adapted for it. Nature's method of procedure—namely, by means of undulating surfaces and outlines of vegetation—will prove our best auxiliary, whether the effect at which we aim be on a large or a small scale. It will, indeed, assist us much to give a constant succession of beautiful combinations, and in respect of land decoration, yield results far surpassing any merely formal arrangement. An undulating surface will be alike preferable, whether for plants of tender growth, those which are mature, or finally those which are in their decline.

> "Pausing at will, our spirits braced, our thoughts
> Pleasant as roses in the thickets blown,
> And pure as dew, bathing their crimson leaves."—*W.*

However diminutive the detail, each subject, every divisional arrangement of decoration should fulfil an object, so as to enhance the general effect. And thus it is that every plant, and each square yard of surface should be made to contribute to the beauty of the soil. In shrubberies, indeed, natural combinations shall best engage attention.

Thus some of the effects mentioned under the head of scenery, may here form a succession, the varieties made use of, and the methods resorted to, being in strict accordance with the circumstances of the case, and the suggestions already given.

When you carefully study the surrounding country, it will commonly provide you with a basis of operation, not only for the general outlines, but also in respect of more detailed arrangements. Should it happen that certain objects subsist out of keeping with the scene, they must be planted out in such wise that they shall not be used as sites. The principal views need to be marked, so as to turn them to the best account. Each outline, then, will become matter for consideration in order to supply its appropriate decoration. In Nature, indeed, we find that, in the valleys, the lowest situation often supplies the principal effect, while in respect of elevated ground the highest peaks prove of chiefest importance. The style in which scenery is treated should, above all things, be true to Nature, instead of being subordinated to false principles. Flower gardens are handled artificially, and objects are placed in formal lines, instead of seeking to conform to Nature's noble balance of irregularity. In natural scenery, indeed, we frequently find the centre low and the boundaries high—a principle which, if carried out in our arrangements, will many times afford scope for bringing distant outlines into view, and promoting a various vegetable growth as well.

The middle line of sight, as I would term it, is always of great moment, as it commonly first challenges attention, and yet, too often, it receives least care. We shall find the compass of frequent use in decoration, in order to enable us to respect the sunshine for the promotion of the general harmony, in accordance with the laws of massing and extent. The size of objects introduced should greatly depend on the amount of space to be decorated; thus, when the ground proves limited, large subjects should be fewer. Trees will subserve many purposes when suitably placed, and where they serve to deepen and strengthen the general impression. In respect of shrubs, the principal effects should be first laid out, after the leading features have been sufficiently considered. For example, there may be a confined path leading through a shrubbery of Portugal Laurel, bright with glistening leaves in winter, charming us with its long white spikes of flowers in spring. The mind, indeed, is so constituted that no one form alone is adequate to impart satisfaction. Nothing suffices short of a suitable succession of harmonious combinations, each yielding noble pleasure in itself, and supplying material for thought. Rests and contrasts, so termed, do not perhaps yield the highest style of beauty, and yet they will be found valuable as accessories, while, by their presence, they promote the satisfaction which we experience from surveying some fair tract arranged according to well determined principles.

The details of the shrubbery will properly consist of promontories, recesses, high grounds, low groups, and boundary lines, each contributing to the general effect. The aspect of the shrubbery should always manifest a due proportion, securing successive displays, and making it requisite to walk over the entire ground in order to see them, and still without losing any sight of distant prospects worth keeping.

Speaking of arrangement, too much stress is occasionally laid upon what people are inclined to like and dislike. Sometimes persons will be found to admire the general effect, while taking exception to the very materials that go to make up the effect. I have known, for instance, those who were vastly pleased with the flowers and shrubs in a foreground, until, perhaps, they caught sight of the Yew some little distance back, and, unaware that the beauty and richness of the flowers were thereby rendered more conspicuous, instantly passed a veto on it as being much too dark. The common Yew, indeed, *Taxus baccata*, makes a capital background. It is also well suited for places where roots of trees abound—places where it will be found to grow and flourish when other evergreens almost entirely disappear. For giving effect in a hollow, it is a tree perhaps the very best adapted of any.

The general effects of shrubbery contain much of what we may term open expanses, foregrounds arranged according to the laws of massing, distant views harmoniously blending with the vegetable groups and boundary lines at hand. Decorative surfaces must be in accordance with the size of the subjects meant to occupy them. A *Sedum*, it is almost needless to observe, will not require the space demanded by a *Sequoia gigantea*. The general outlines must be in unison with the immediate surroundings, outline blending with outline. Bold planting is sometimes spoiled from the circumstance that the lines of distance, as visible from sites for observation, have not been duly considered, evoking results quite out of character, so that the results are actually worse than if no attempt at decoration had been made; for, as already stated, all our arrangements must be in conformity with the general scenery around. Above all, we must avoid reducing undulating ground to a mere railway level. The natural soil, indeed, has always surfaces more or less concave. In rising ground these, catching the water, hold it in reserve for the hot weather. In all arrangements we must complete an effect, and *unite* it with another.

RECESSES PARTICULAR.

In shrubberies recesses may subsist to an almost unlimited extent, and are found to contribute to effect more than what is commonly supposed; indeed, they seem particularly adapted for the development of some special beauty of vegetable life. The term, particular recesses, would include the different sorts of gardens, such as the Rosery, Rockery, and the like. The development of a particular beauty should always be the leading object in each recess, and these should be divided so as to produce a succession of pleasing impressions on the mind, so as each to be correct in feeling with the other.

> "Ah, what a sweet recess, thought I, is here,
> Instantly throwing down my limbs at ease
> Upon a bed of heath; full many a spot
> Of hidden beauty have I chanced to espy
> Among the mountains—never one like this,
> So lonesome and so perfectly secure.
> Not melancholy, no, for it is green,
> And bright, and fertile, furnished in itself
> With the few needful things that life requires,
> In rugged arms, how soft it seems to lie,
> How tenderly protected. Far and near
> We have an image of the pristine earth,
> The planet in its nakedness; were this
> Man's only dwelling, sole appointed seat,
> First, last, and single, in the breathing world,
> It could not be more quiet—peace is here."*

Recesses ought to be arranged so as to enhance the general effect in conformity with the natural character of the scenery. Undulating ground yields much scope for the production of harmonious combinations, no two recesses being necessarily alike. Thus, with

* Wordsworth.

each succeeding year, the progressively maturing outlines of our plants will shed charms ever renewed on the surrounding scene, so that a few acres may come to yield an almost infinite diversity of form, and light, and shade, and marvels in fine of vegetable life. Thus every form of growth, each particular effect, should evoke perfections of its own, perfections never to be forgotten, fountains of pleasant memories, wellsprings of gladsome thoughts, making us feel better and happier, raising us above wearying cares, and filling our hearts with the sunshine of life.

It will be understood that a recess should not be a mere hole cut in a wood, or a promontory, like a clump tacked on to a plantation; for subjects should blend together so as to form a harmonious whole. Indeed, the immense variety of forms, which the vegetable kingdom displays, has too often led to the employment of contrasts that but disparage the scenery, and yet, perhaps, are held up as models of arrangement. The individual plants may please, but the general effect must fail to satisfy.

As respects arrangement, each structure should have as good a position as is compatible with the area of the soil. Those who attend greenhouses soon become aware that certain plants thrive better in one position than another. The hardy vegetation that subsists in the open, will be found not less discriminating as regards light, soil, and water. Errors in decoration are often committed by reason of aiming at too great straightness and uniformity. Undesirable extremes are much too prevalent; some object, perhaps, being situated so as to charm us with its loveliness, while others, which may be immediately contiguous, are at once harsh and incongruous. Such things ought not to be. Extremes should only be had resort to in exceptional instances, and in strict subserviency to the character of the scene. Lightness, grace, majesty, or whatever character is intended, should be realised.

ROSETUM.

A Rosery, be it large or small, will hold a place in most gardens. It will properly occupy some convenient recesses contiguous to the mansion. The Rose needs no encomium from me. Its grace and loveliness, along with its ineffable fragrance, are simply the admiration of the world. Many of these beautiful flowers, as now cultivated, however, are better adapted for the embellishment of an exhibition than suited to a garden, so brief is their duration, and so few are the flowers, taking into consideration the size of the plant. Roses that yield the finest blooms, and that last a long time in flower, will be found best suited for cultivation. How delightful is the *Rosa indica* (the old monthly China), which remaining with us so long after its kindred have disappeared reminds us in December of the sunny days of June. During a visit to various places in England and Belgium in the October of 1871, I saw no outside flowers so abundant as this. In the Royal Botanic Gardens at Brussels there were some small beds thinly filled with plants of the China Rose, visible a long way off. The effect was charming in the extreme: that the plants had been for some time in bloom was evident from the seed-vessels; and yet there were many still unopened buds, which would probably continue to unfold until the frost should stay their career.

The Roses most recently cultivated are rather smaller in size of plants than is desirable. In other respects, too, a Rosery is incomplete without climbing Roses, which are so well calculated to set off the delicate beauty of the plants. Climbing varieties, in fact, should be included in every Rosery, along with specimens of the *Jasminum nudiflorum*, so well adapted by its summer leafage and its floral winter effects. Some few years will be needed fully to establish the various climbers to combine with the Roses, but meanwhile they do no harm.

Where the winter proves too cold, the more tender varieties may be taken down and arranged in bundles. In order to do this, their early growth must be carefully attended to, so that the branches shall be left free. In some places they may even be strawed up where they grow, at least where this does not prove objectionable. Occasionally the roots may be slated over, so as to keep off water, as with the Noisette and Tea-Scented Roses. Numerous localities, however, subsist in Britain where these expedients are uncalled for.

Many plants there are which neither in summer nor winter detract in the least from the loveliness of the Rose. Thus the light foliage of the *Betula alba pendula* will be found in some cases to answer admirably. The *Ailantus glandulosa*, *Spiræa Lindleyana*, the *Acer Negundo variegatum*, and others will enhance the lustre of our rosery. Strong contrasting hues such as those of the *Calceolaria* and the Scarlet Pelargonium must, however, be avoided. A Rosery should be a scene of *delicate beauty*.

In soil where there is much diversity of outline, also where temples, columns, arbours, arches, verandahs, festoons, and the like abound, climbers may be resorted to with charming results. There is a rich variety—as, the Rose, Jasmine, the *Passiflora, Aristolochia, Ampelopsis, Vitis, Wistaria, Hedera, Cotoneaster, Pyracantha, Cydonia, Tecoma,* and the *Humulus* to choose from. The great success achieved by Mr. Jackman with the Clematis is well known. Indeed one might discourse at length on the numerous effects that climbing plants are capable of realising. Temples, arbours, summer-houses, resting-places, should be always in suitable situations, so as to enable those who resort to them to discover scenery worthy of admiration.

Climbers will form an admirable scene themselves, giving a feeling of enchantment. A book might be filled with a description of the effects of festoons and arches in the low grounds, temples, colonnades, and verandahs forming irregular outlines on the high ground, arbours and columns intercombining the whole length together by their introduction into various parts of the scenery. Vases would be useful for various hardy trailing plants. In these scenes *Sedums, Saxifragas,* and the like are proper to take the place of grass in suitable undulations, and will keep the whole in true character for perpetual beauty.

The *Rhododendron* is well suited to be the principal of a large recess. This can be seen in various parts of the country, its undulating masses giving beautiful grays in the distance, various lights and shades of green in the foreground, with beautiful elliptical leaves arranged in rosettes on the branches.

These plants are well adapted for bold, undulating valleys, the outlines being assisted by such plants as the *Abies Douglasii,* with the *Picea nobilis* crowning the highest ground. The variegated forms of the *Taxus,* &c., may assist the permanent effects of the plants themselves, and the ground can be covered with flowering-plants at different periods, such as the *Cotoneaster* and *Vinca* assisting the ground lines. The noble heads of flowers of the Rhododendron should be fully developed, keeping the masses of white or light colour on the highest mounds, the purples in the hollows (a little common yew would assist these effects), and the scarlets in the intermediate lines. Thus the scene would be made complete, and when these plants put forth their own special beauties they will produce an effect of *richness* such as shall be a "household word."

Undulations will often permit us to compass many and most pleasing arrangements that would otherwise prove impracticable. With respect to fruiting plants, the effects of some are charming in the extreme, while all afford materials for interest as well as wonder. The *Berberis vulgaris* has the loveliest autumnal light intense scarlet berries; the Rowan tree is a miracle of beauty when covered with its dark scarlet fruitage; while the dark berries of the *Cotoneaster obtusa, C. affinis* (see the Royal Gardens, Kew, in autumn), and many varieties of *Cratægus* display others of most varied hues.

Quaint results might often be accomplished with plants, such as varieties of the genera *Berberis, Ilex, Pernettya, Cydonia, Rubus, Juniperus, Smilax,* and *Ruscus*.

Numerous facilities for realising scenes of loveliness subsist in almost every pleasure-ground—facilities which, were they only fitly turned to account, would evoke results the most delightful. A fine specimen of *Ribes sanguinea*, when viewed in springtide, often proves a most delightful object, and, at the same time, does not interfere with other growths. Too rarely, however, is its beauty adequately recognised, or that of some other plants which often have the appearance of being placed in shrubberies without any particular object, either to grow or to be seen; and yet, by studying Nature's laws and making her principles in some degree our own, wonders might be achieved in years to come such as are now hardly dreamed of.

The very loveliest combinations might be produced in spring with the purple and yellow *Cytisus Laburnum*, and *Cratægus* or Hawthorn; these having climbers attached to each plant when planted could have many effects.

The *Cerasus*, or common Laurel, forms, along with the *Magnolia, Andromeda, Phillyrea, Hydrangea, Euonymus, Elæagnus,* and *Daphne*, scenes such as may be called truly admirable. Even when neglected they look beautiful. They cost but little, and, once fairly established, last for years.

Of all the lovely forms of vegetable life with which this world is blessed, none, perhaps, are more strongly calculated to elicit our warmest admiration than the many varieties of the Lily tribe or form. They are indeed among the joys of earth. For large spaces or for small they are alike adapted. Nothing, perhaps, will prove more charming for an amateur than a Lily garden. Festooned with climbers, it will be replete with loveliness, fill the air with fragrance, and the heart with joy. To the *Liliaceæ* belong many of the flowers that gladden us in spring and summer, proving in all their varied aspects sources of unalloyed gratification. Some of them will even unite the old year with the new. Taking in the plants of the flowing leafage, a larger scope will be given, as the *Tritoma Uvaria, Eranthis hyemalis,* or winter Aconite, the *Galanthus nivalis* (Snowdrop), and others. Many of the following genera, as the *Yucca, Veratrum, Dracæna australis, Arum, Hemerocallis,* and *Agapanthus,* the latter with its bright blue October umbels, prove well adapted for a Lily garden. Again, the *Schizostylis coccinea* displays masses of brilliant scarlet flowers far on in the winter months; while grasses, should we use them, will set off delicate outlines, and *Scolopendriums* and *Funkias* are adapted for bolder ones. The *Czackia Liliastrum* suits well the foreground, and there are many others of aspect no less varied than charming, which it is hardly needful to name here in detail. The hardy variety of *Bambusais,* most graceful in aspect, its light stems waving in every passing breeze, will serve well to unite the ground lines of plants with the taller growths of trees in gardens of the flowering line.

In respect of gaining a knowledge of forms, we shall find that a day spent alone with Nature, midst vales and hills, will often do much to inspire us with a true feeling of what our outlines ought to be. In Nature, indeed, we witness effects the most diversified, and acquire a knowledge that no book suffices to impart. The aspects of plants vary according to their arrangement. The light and airy character of many summer grasses, now becoming better known, renders them most effective, and gullies of moist strong land, especially where undulations subsist, may be very suitably occupied by grasses large and small. Indeed, pathways in gullies might be nearly encircled by the Pampas grass in conjunction with the *Bambusa,* and smaller grasses, thus producing scenes the most charming and diversified in fineness of foliage.

I remember once being greatly struck with the *Genista æthnensis* in Glasnevin gardens, its grass-like foliage hanging from its somewhat rugged stems, laden with a perfect profusion of golden flowers.

A rockery, when constructed, as it occasionally is, in some large recess, the angular outlines of the stone work blending with those of the plants, is sometimes productive of most interesting results. In hollows, and where the soil is much varied, a liberal use of veiling plants, properly used, will hold up the soil, and even prevent stones from being necessary where stones are scarce. The ground itself, as it were, produces the effects by its undulation, its form uniting masses of Alpine plants. The costly system of carting heaps of soil, or of massing roots of trees together, need not be resorted to; for by lowering the land in one place it is easy to raise it in another, and produce undulations cheaply. Messrs. Backhouse & Son's Rockery, at the York Nurseries will give an illustration of this. Rooteries are sometimes made as substitutes for rockeries, producing fearfully unnatural appearance, and certainly showing more cruelty than beauty. An old root blown over in woodland scenery and covered over with such plants as *Polypodium vulgare* would not be out of place; but to see hundreds of roots carted together for making romantic or rockery scenes appears to me to be a memorial of contempt for noble trees.

Walks, where the scenery is romantic, should be provided with winding turns, so as to yield varying glimpses of the landscape, each in character to the scene. Water is almost absolutely essential to the romance of the scene. Running waters especially are sure to charm from the first moment their low murmur is heard. Whether hurrying along in a series of cascades, or sparkling perchance in some rocky bed or leafy thicket, they yield a bright store of life. Every variation of *outline* or *surface* of its bed gives a particular effect to water, therefore always seek a proportion of these two.

> "High or low appeared no trace
> Of motion, save the water that descended,
> Diffused, adown that barrier of steep rock;
> And softly creeping like a breath of air,
> Such as is sometimes seen and hardly seen
> To brush the still breast of a crystal lake."—*Wordsworth.*

Hanging over the water we may have varieties of the Fir tribe, *Pinus sylvestris* (Scotch Fir), which has a rich effect over clear water; climbers, too, will cover the rocks with garlands fair and gay. Sometimes we may have bridges, stepping-stones, and islands, together with objects of varied interest. Flowers and plants of perfume, suitably disposed—Lavender, Jasmine, Pinks, Sweetbrier, Wallflower, and others—these arranged so as not to interfere with the Alpine flowers; in fine, a perfect wilderness of sweets should likewise fill the air with fragrance. Lakes or ponds, where they subsist, will afford many facilities for effects of quaintness. (See Figure of Water Outlines).

CHAPTER IV.

NATURAL PARKS—STYLE.

Park scenery displays its alternating masses and extent in the groups and outlines of trees and other forms. These, with grassy glades alternating in light and shade, must be arranged all in true character with its beauty. As the principal object aimed at in parks, however, is the fitting exhibition of the various forms and hues of tree-life, other lines of sight, so termed, must be rendered subservient to these. It is especially needful that the natural principles on which effective arrangements depend, should be most carefully attended to. The first basis for our operations will need to be attentively considered. A due regard to the outlines of the surrounding country, as bearing on park effects, is essential. Considerable advantage will be gained by the study of mountain scenery, followed by that of the quieter details of comparatively level ground. By so doing, the mind learns to form a just conception of the principles of arrangement and design, thus opening up many a fruitful source of pleasure and of profit as well. It will also prove further desirable to survey the best accessible examples of well arranged park scenery, and with our own eyes see how Art has succeeded in vying with Nature. Tollymore Park, already adverted to, and Viscount Annesley's estate, yield admirable illustrations in point. The outlines of the woods in Tollymore Park, County Down, are all in harmony with those of the hills beyond, while in the demesne at Castlewellan it is otherwise. Both these parks, however, will be found well worthy of inspection. At Tollymore, the outlines of the woods are in comparison with the mountain outlines, thus causing the scenery to impress the mind. Castlewellan grounds always inspire admiration. Still they have not the power to impress their beauty on the mind as the scenery of Tollymore—the outlines of the woods not being in harmony with the mountains.

Approaches, shaded by trees as above, the distinctive outlines of each being plainly discernible, are of great importance contiguous to the mansion. Otherwise, stretches of undulating turf often yield rests the most delightful in park scenery. Nothing, indeed, can well be more effective than the fair outlines of deciduous trees and noble contours of the Fir tribe, particularly when in strict keeping with the size of the place and the character of the surroundings. Often we may have in one place a quiet valley, in another some romantic glen, or wild moorland scene. Numberless, in truth, are the results achievable by means of arrangements conformable to the requirements of the soil, clothing it as thus with beauties infinite. When too great a sameness however prevails, it prevents the natural features from being as clearly discernible as they would otherwise prove. Still, in spite of this occasional sameness, the parks of England display, in many instances, a perfect wealth of loveliness. No person, perhaps, accomplished more in aid of park decoration than did Gilpin. The style which he adopted was extremely well suited for the so-termed Round-headed trees of his day. It was, indeed, a great advance on the straight lines of avenue cut right through the vegetation and endeavouring to make streets of vegetation, as it were, but without any sufficient reason for this straightness being apparent. Regularity seems wanted for the body of man, but irregularity in quantity and form for noble thoughts are required for the mind.

Where to plant and where not to plant, can only be decided, generally speaking, on the ground itself. Heights, for numerous reasons, will nearly always need to be planted. The advantages afforded by a judicious and natural distribution of outlines, are fully appreciated even by the lower animals, which often spend a great portion of their time in sheltered recesses. In such, indeed, are found in rich abundance the earliest and latest grasses. Natural planting increases the number of outlines, and yields by much the greatest diversity. If only we ascend a mountain slope, what a difference becomes discernible when once the line of tree-life is passed. Even in the midst of scenes the most magnificent, a sense of barrenness is experienced.

Animal life, as subsisting in parks, is often very beautiful—life in motion in the midst of what is stationary life gives a fertile aspect to the soil; it also assists the mind to judge of love and cheerfulness, by seeing an unknown size compared with one well known, and if only water be present, the graceful harmony of the whole is very greatly intensified.

Straight avenues should very rarely be resorted to. They are, in fact, ill adapted for setting off vegetable growths. When one enters a straight avenue, at first but three or four trees are visible, and the idea directly gains ground that all the trees are alike. Whereas when looked at to the inside of a curve (the line of massing) they all show perfect outlines even as far as the eye is able to distinguish them. These street-avenues are sometimes constructed under the impression that some great effect is produced, and yet a little reflection must, I think, convince any one that for natural scenery they are about one of the worst forms imaginable. The natural laws of massing and extent produce results as diverse from those which ensue from the use of hard straight lines as truth is superior to falsehood.

In natural planting, every feature of the surroundings, worthy of it, may be set forth, while that which is not worthy may be concealed. Nothing, indeed, need be lost that ought to be retained. And by only acting conformably to the natural principles of decoration, we shall secure more impressive displays in the distant views, while each single yard of ground, so to speak, shall be found to yield its distinct effects. If the surroundings be good, numberless desirable combinations, large and small, will be visible. Examples of these straight avenues, concerning the merits of which I have ventured to give so decided an opinion, are to be seen in many parts of the country, even in places where every facility subsists for carrying out the natural principles of planting. Generally speaking, for developing leading effects, something more will be requisite than merely planting the higher ground with lofty forms and low situations with smaller ones. Masses of vegetation should display gradations of light and shade with gentle undulations. Small elevations are much embellished by trees of graceful aspect. Many of the Coniferæ are of extreme beauty, but they ought to be arranged with a view to effect, and not be merely dotted here and there over the surface. In some parts of the world they rise to an elevation far exceeding anything to be witnessed in these countries, producing, indeed, the grandest effects. Pinetums are of very great value, for by their means we become aware which plants will reach their proper size and which will not. Through the kindness of proprietors, experimental grounds of this description are open to the public whereby they may become acquainted with many valuable specimens, and the way in which they may be made to contribute embellishment.

Park scenery should exhibit a variety of distinctive features. Where the scenery is extensive, bold masses of rock prove most picturesque. Where, however, rocks do not abound, open spaces amid the woods on hill sides will be found to contrast advantageously with the dark tints of the tree stems. Generally speaking, however, the woods and waters abound with materials of beauty which only need to be suitably handled in order to yield the fairest results.

As regards roads in parks, they may be broadly divided into public and private. Drives that lead from the main road to the dwelling should be decorated accordingly; more private drives, on the other hand, being made with a view to exhibiting scenery should be arranged over the best sites for seeing the scenery. Roads amid natural scenery should never be constructed to show off their own perfections merely, nor should vegetation, which is the very soul of all our arrangements, pay tribute to the road. Where there is fine old timber, it will be best to make the foreground suit the trees rather than the converse. Roads should curve boldly round rising grounds, and wind gracefully through leafy thickets in pleasant alternation, while here and there will be found an avenue, recess, or effect of some sort, or a mass of some tree of aspect more than commonly charming—for example, the *Pyrus Aucuparia* (or Mountain Ash) in all its rich array of autumn fruitage.

> "The mountain ash,
> Decked with autumnal berries that outshine
> Spring's richest blossoms, yields a splendid show
> Amid the leafy woods; and ye have seen
> By a brook side or solitary tarn
> How she her station doth adorn, the pool
> Flows at her feet, and all the gloomy rocks
> Are brightened round her."

It may be observed in passing, that it is well worth while going to see how joyously the birds alight to partake of the feast which Nature has so bountifully provided for them. But to return, very much might be said about the picturesque loveliness of the Oak, *Quercus pedunculata;* and the "joyous Elm," *Ulmus campestris,* and the sweet Chestnut, *Castanea vesca,* will give a most sedate noble effect. In respect of forest scenery, no two pieces of ground will be found quite alike; and when once the natural principles of decoration are thoroughly understood, we shall be better able to deal with the various effects that may be produced. How beautiful these in many cases are, may be seen in our numberless parks wherein but a few varieties of round-headed trees are found, and still capable of producing the pleasantest impression, leaving many a gladsome memory behind.

> "From whose calm centre thou through height or depth
> May'st penetrate wherever truth shall lead."

CHAPTER V.

TOWN PARKS.

In these days of progress, when a more or less complete knowledge of scientific principles is diffused among all classes, new ideas spring forth, and fresh wants make themselves felt. The increasing desire for the construction of parks where the life and grace of Nature may be realised, yields evidence of this. Vegetable structures, as is well known, will subsist for the most part in all the places where man himself abides, shedding a charm on his surroundings to which even the most commonplace are not insensible. It is not, however, alone sufficient to ensure the health of towns to have a piece of decorated ground accessible to the inhabitants: abundance of fresh air and pure water are absolute essentials. How important these are may be seen from the present construction of towns, wherein for one good street we shall too often find ten bad ones—ill paved, ill drained, and ill lighted, in fact, perfect nurseries of discomfort and disease.

And yet, parks displaying features the most pleasing, yielding recreation and enjoyment throughout the year, might be made within easy distance of all towns.

The shrubs employed in decoration should be most effective, the choice being a matter of considerable importance. There should also be a good display of carpeting plants in full accordance with the different scenes. As much diversity as is consistent with the undulation of the ground and general surroundings, should be always aimed at. Existing undulations should be made the most of, while, at the same time, all violent extremes must be avoided. We need not cut up the surface on the one hand, or level it on the other, but rather assist the curvature of Nature.

Every accessible water supply should be rendered available; it will be found to impart life and soul to our efforts. Here the brightest colours that harmonise should be introduced, for impressions the most vivid are desirable.

Hardy vegetation should receive all requisite care and attention, inasmuch as its beauty endures for years. Climbers are productive of many lovely effects, and some which are trained round windows in the West End of London far surpass in grace and beauty those in any park I have seen near London. Numerous, in truth, are the growths of this kind suitable for parks. The *Robinia*, if planted in some dell, for example, is truly admirable. Then there are the Weeping Birch, numerous varieties of Maple, well known to be good town trees, and some of the more late introduced varieties would be well worth rearing, *e.g.*, the Rhododendron, which thrive well in sheltered spots, and are beautiful indeed. A reserve ground outside large towns, to which plants that had not set their buds might be removed, their places meanwhile replaced by others, is most desirable; a complete glow of beauty might be had cheaply in their season of flowering. In other respects, the roads should be arranged with regard to convenience, making them, however, subservient to the display of every beauty of scenery and vegetation. Where large spaces are required for equitation, outdoor games and the like, the trees immediately about ought to receive special attention and care. Plans for town parks should be drawn up in accordance with natural principles, as well as other styles of horticulture works of Art. Yet, how frequently do we hear it said, this is a nice plan, without a single remark upon what makes its niceness.

These parks being for use throughout the entire year, a perpetual effect is really necessary to give satisfaction, and the time of the succession of effects must be most carefully studied; therefore, the natural principle of arrangement of scenery will be the best, instead of any packing system it is possible to invent.

CHAPTER VI.

WOODLANDS

Timber ground in the neighbourhood of mansions has walks made through it, occasionally miles in length. These are commonly taken through parts where cover is wanted for game, or where it is desirable to admit air to the trees. It is often, however, found troublesome to protect ornamental trees and shrubs from the game. Mr. Brown, in his excellent work, enlarges very forcibly on the undesirability of harbouring game at all.

In woodland scenery an effort should always be made to realise pleasing combinations. The *Salix*, with its coloured stems, the scarlet-hued dogwood often serve to enliven a bosquet otherwise too sombre. Picturesque trees already subsisting, some grand old oak with gnarled stem and twisted branches, should be carefully cherished. The indigenous Flora, naturally so lovely, will be greatly set off by varieties of strong growing herbaceous plants.

As a basis for woodland decoration, the *Rhododendron* is admirably well suited. We must, however, bear in mind that the middle line of sight will furnish us with very valuable material for decorative purposes. The common Yew, as already mentioned, adapts itself most capitally to hollows, as does the *Buxus* to high situations.

In woodland scenery, we find that those plants which held but a secondary place in shrubbery assume a position of much importance. How frequently do we witness the most striking scenes in open spaces, bright glades where tree and bush and flower all blend in harmony together. The light foliage, it may be, droops on some emerald bank, while, here and there, spring up the sweetest woodland flowers.

The plants we are to employ as a basis must depend on the formation of the ground, difficult to find in every way; but by consulting this, we may often realise results the most pleasing and diversified. The *Tritoma Uvaria*, many large varieties of grasses, as also the *Epilobium angustifolium*, prove most serviceable in decoration. The Laburnum, the Syringa, *Sambucus*, *Ribes*, if only planted in accordance with natural principles, all impart charms of their own. The pendent flowers of the *Ribes*, indeed, are beautiful as they are welcome in early spring. In sheltered spots, during a mild season, the green leaf will often linger even till the period when the new buds begin to swell.

It will sometimes prove advantageous to select a suitable piece of ground at the extremity of woodland in order to the display of perhaps a special beauty of scenery or form of vegetation, and thus furnish a motive for going thitherward. Sometimes in ground of this description we may light upon a favoured spot, some dell, perhaps, where trees lend amplest shelter, and where frost scarcely ever penetrates. Here the vegetation, protected from cold and wind, flourishes so as to astonish and delight the beholder with its delicate and graceful forms. Many plants, otherwise strangers, such as varieties of the *Robinia* and Indian *Rhododendron*, might even be naturalised in places of this kind, and so unfold their loveliness. Temples, so termed, or leafy bowers, are useful as a refuge in case of sudden rainfalls at a distance from the house. Dells, again, where we can have running waters or crystal pools whose quiet depths mirror the waving foliage are perfectly delightful. Should this on the distant high ground be surrounded by the giant Beeches *(Fagus sylvaticus)*, which in their age have a pendulous character in their lower branches, taking a wildly acute form at their summits, the irregular natural ground between these and the water might have its promontories planted with the *Salix babylonica*, whose effect is as Wordsworth describes it—

> "The willow weeping trees twinkling hoar
> Glanced oft upturned along the breezy shore,
> Low bending o'er the coloured water, fold
> The moveless boughs and leaves like threads of gold."

The rough hollows beyond might be planted with *Fraxinus excelsior pendula*, Weeping Ash, from some prominent pieces of land entering into the water; *Ulmus montana pendula* hangs her craw-like branches giving a peculiar effect at the water's side. Masses of the *Fagus pendula* would unite the lower Weeping trees to the Beeches surrounding the scene, and a very few *Betula alba pendula* might be used to assist to develop the effects.

> "To mark the birches stems all golden light
> That lit the dark slant woods with silvery white."

As too many Birches would give too light an impression to the scene, and thus destroy its character, other Weeping plants might be used according to the wants of the landscape. One or two Lombardy Poplars would be advantageous to give life to the effects.

CHAPTER VII.

PINETUM.

Among the Evergreens introduced of late years are numerous specimens of the Fir tribe. Often these plants were quite new, and it was therefore most desirable to ascertain what effect the climate might have on their growth and development ere they were employed in decoration. This knowledge has mainly accrued through the kindness of possessors of property, and thus it is that beautiful plants previously unknown to us are available. With their soft green tints, they remind one of summer when summer has fled, and in their enduring loveliness recal the poet's happy thought—

"A thing of beauty is a joy for ever."

Plants of the Fir tribe, nevertheless, are seldom arranged in such fashion as to elicit all the noble effects of which they are capable. The health-giving property of Firs, indeed, is well known. The growth of these plants, in fact, seems, as it were, a sort of criterion of the purity of the atmosphere. They will not even live in towns, at least as at present constructed.

Firs afford excellent protection, and shelter a dwelling admirably from cold winds. Their towering groups are full of majesty. Our choice, of course, will much depend on circumstances. The *Pinus austriaca* is very suitable for low-lying boundaries, while the *Abies* will be found to accord with higher ground. To the majestic aspect of the Cedar of Lebanon and matchless elegance of the *Deodara*, I have more than once already adverted. Then we have the quiet grace of the acutely drooping foliage from the upright branches of *Pinus Sabiniana*, also the impressive outlines of the *Taxus baccata fastigiata*, the purity of *Pinus excelsa*, and a multitude of others more or less adapted to embellish recesses, avenues, and other expanses. The silver-like effect of *Picea nobilis*, suitable for promontories, may be witnessed at Castle Kennedy and other places—firm amid the versatile breeze that blows in all directions the plants on every side. It is not requisite to complain that the Pine tints are too dark hued, for much diversity of light and shade will in reality be found to subsist, adaptable to every purpose, and enhancing the ineffable grace and loveliness of Nature.

Advertisements.

REGISTERED FOR TRANSMISSION ABROAD.

THE
GARDENERS' CHRONICLE
(ESTABLISHED 1841),·

A Weekly Illustrated Journal,

DEVOTED TO ALL BRANCHES OF HORTICULTURE & ALLIED SUBJECTS.

Published every Friday, Price Fivepence; Post-free, 5½d.

THE object of the "GARDENERS' CHRONICLE" is to diffuse the fullest, earliest, and most authentic information on the subjects on which it treats.

It is designed to convey intelligence to its readers on all matters connected with **Gardening and Practical Natural History**; to supply the requirements of COUNTRY GENTLEMEN, GARDENERS, and AMATEURS OF ALL CLASSES; and to form a **Medium of Intercommunication** between all persons at home or abroad taking an interest in cultural pursuits.

The **Contributors** include the ablest and most trustworthy writers, the most experienced practitioners, and the most eminent scientific men in their several departments.

Original Illustrations of subjects of interest to those engaged in gardening, natural history, or rural pursuits generally, are freely given.

ALL SUBSCRIPTIONS PAYABLE IN ADVANCE.

THE UNITED KINGDOM:
3 Months, 6s; 6 Months, 11s 11d; 12 Months, £1 3s 10d.

FOREIGN SUBSCRIPTIONS,
INCLUDING POSTAGE FOR TWELVE MONTHS:
Australia, Belgium, Canada, France, Jamaica, New Zealand, West Indies, United States, £1 6s 0d.

Austria, China, Holland, India, Portugal, Prussia, Spain, Switzerland, £1 10s. 4d. Russia, Italy, Denmark, £1 14s 8d.

P. O. O. to be made payable at the King Street Post Office, London, to WILLIAM RICHARDS.

PUBLISHING AND ADVERTISING OFFICE:—
41, WELLINGTON STREET, COVENT GARDEN, LONDON, W.C.

Advertisements.

THE DROMORE PATENT HEATING COMPANY
(LIMITED),
40, LOWER ORMOND QUAY, DUBLIN.

COWAN'S PATENT COMPENSATING SYSTEM
FOR
HEATING ALL KINDS OF BUILDINGS BY HOT WATER,
Saves the Entire Cost of Fuel.

LIST OF PLACES where Apparatuses have already been erected, with Extracts from Letters received concerning them. Several of these have been forwarded to us by the Gentlemen for whom the Apparatuses have been erected, but the majority are from Gardeners and others by whom they are worked. Most of the letters will be found in full in our illustrated Pamphlet, which will be forwarded post free on application,

NAME.	ADDRESS.	EXTRACTS FROM LETTERS.
The Marquis of SALISBURY	Hatfield, Herts	It is a decided success, and more cannot be said in its favour.
Lord DONERAILE	Doneraile, Co. Cork	I am convinced that for steady temperature and cleanliness it cannot be surpassed.
The Earl of SHANNON	Castle Martyr, Co. Cork	A continuous heat is obtained, and first rate lime produced, which fully compensates for the fuel consumed and the attendance required.
Lord CLANMORRIS	Creg Clare, Co. Galway	We have the range heated free, and a profit besides.
Lord MIDDLETON	Birdsall House, York	I am glad to tell you that the Limekiln is heating magnificently. . . . . I shall be glad to show and recommend your grand system of heating to anyone.
MITCHEL HENRY, Esq., M.P.	Kylemore Castle, Co. Galway	It has, indeed, surpassed my most sanguine expectation. . . . . Not only have I the heat for nothing, but a considerable profit.
A. WAUCHOPE, Esq.	Niddrie House, near Edinburgh	We have ample heat, and that most steady, also a fine quality of Lime, which will not only pay the cost of fuel, but realize a handsome profit.
JOHN T. GRAY, Esq.	Temple Hill, Blackrock, Co. Dublin	The System is satisfactory in the highest degree, and cannot be too highly recommended.
T. G. MESSENGER, Esq., Horticultural Builder.	Loughborough	I have just got the first boiler to work on your System, and it appears perfectly successful.
Major MOLONY	Killtanon, Tulla, Co. Clare	I see good practical results from the Apparatus you have lately put up here.
J. T. D. CROSBIE, Esq.	Ardfert Abbey, Tralee	The Apparatus erected here is a complete success.
Messrs. J. & R. THYNE	Nurserymen, Glasgow	So far everything goes well and perfectly satisfactory. . . The Lime is pronounced first class.
H. D. EVANS, Esq.	Highmead, Llanybyther, Wales	Your system of heating has proved a complete success.
The Rev. Mr. TOLLEMACHE	The Rectory, South Wytham, Grantham	The heat is magnificent, and I like the Apparatus very much.
DAVID RITCHIE, Esq.	Fifeshire	The Kiln is doing very well. . . . . I will write you, and give the gain through the use of the Kiln.

Illustrated Pamphlets, with full particulars, post free on Application as above.

Advertisements.

HORTICULTURAL
IRON AND WIRE WORKS.

MANUFACTURER & CONTRACTOR
FOR ALL KINDS OF
IRON AND WIRE WORK
(PLAIN AND ORNAMENTAL)

FOR GARDENS AND CONSERVATORIES.
GARDEN ESPALIERS, SQUARES, AND CORDONS.
GARDEN WALL WIRING,
On the most Improved Principles for Strength, Durability, and Neatness.
(SPECIALITY.)
**COVERED WAY ESPALIERS, GARDEN ARCHWAYS,
ROSE FENCES, ROSARIES, RABBIT-PROOF GARDEN FENCING.
GARDEN BORDERING.**
LAWN AVIARIES AND PHEASANTRIES.
CONSERVATORIES fitted up with Wrought-Iron Flower Stage Stands, and Wire-Work Flower Stands, Suspending Baskets, Trellis Work for Creepers, Aviaries, &c.
Vineries and other Fruit Houses fitted up with Strained Wire Trellises.
WROUGHT-IRON ENTRANCE AND GARDEN GATES.
WROUGHT AND CAST-IRON RAILING.
Plain and Ornamental Verandahs, in Cast-Iron, Wrought-Iron, and Wire.

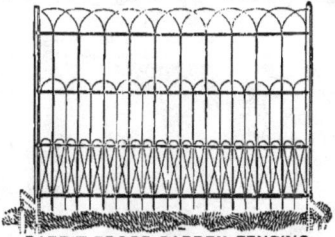

RABBIT PROOF GARDEN FENCING.

R. HOLLIDAY,
2A, PORTOBELLO TERRACE, NOTTING HILL GATE,
LONDON, W.
(Close to High Street, Notting Hill.)

Advertisements.

ECONOMY IN FUEL.
MUSGRAVE'S PATENT SLOW COMBUSTION STOVES.
IMPROVED UNDER A THIRD PATENT.
For heating Conservatories, Vineries, Churches, Private Houses, and Public Buildings. Will burn for Six Months without re-lighting.

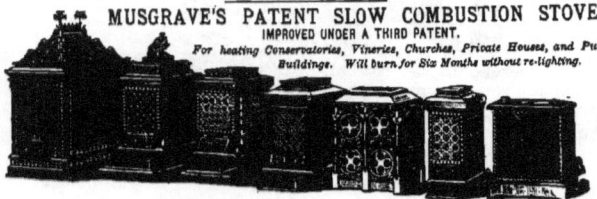

MUSGRAVE & Co. beg to refer to the following extract from an article by Shirley Hibberd, Esq., in the *Floral World*, as a proof of the efficiency of these stoves:—

"Requiring a heating apparatus for a lean-to, twenty-four feet by nine feet, sufficient to keep out frost, I tried one of Musgrave's Patent Stoves. It answered to perfection from the very first, gives a heat as sweet and steady as hot water, occasions less trouble than any similar plan of heating we have ever had to do with, and is evidently the very thing that was required for portable houses, for it need not touch the soil at all—and certainly requires no kind of fixing in it. The house in which this stove is placed has a sunk path along the back, and a raised border of earth along the front. The stove is a handsome piece of furniture, and occupies a place in the centre of the house. As this is a *slow combustion* stove, it must be so placed as to ensure a good draught; granting which, I have no hesitation in pronouncing it a most useful and valuable invention."

EXTRACTS FROM A LARGE NUMBER OF UNSOLICITED TESTIMONIALS:

From Captain Brooke, J.P., Templepatrick.

GENTLEMEN,—I got one of your Greenhouse Stoves with a water chamber about six years since, which wants relining with fire-brick.

The bricks are 8½ x 4in., and it will take twenty to do it. I think the price of the Stove was £4 10s. The Stove has proved so efficient that I have recommended it to all my friends who wish to preserve their plants during the winter, for, with the attention of my gardener, it has preserved mine through some very severe frosts, and enabled me in the spring-time to supply cuttings to gardeners less fortunate, although they had expensive flues to heat their houses.

My greenhouse is 26 feet x 12, and the stove is placed in the centre under the stageing, with an upright iron flue, through the glass roof, and has never given me any trouble.

From John P. Williams, Esq., Exchequer and Audit Department, Somerset House.

More than 10 years since, I had one of your Slow Combustion Stoves, and which has been in constant use in my greenhouse for the whole of that time. It has been a perfect success, and has kept my plants safe in the severest winters.

From John Bellows, Esq., Gloucester.

Kindly send me another Stove. This will make the fifth Stove I shall have had of you. I am pleased beyond all expectation with them. Three of your No. 4 size warm my large printing office—nearly 100,000 cubic feet of air, and with a roof containing a large quantity of glass much exposed to cold. They are so perfectly under control that we keep the temperature exactly what we please to have it, and with a pure ventilation and freedom from draught. I consider I am under a debt to you for so perfect an invention.

HEATING BY HOT WATER.
HOT WATER STOVE.

To be used in connexion with a Hot Water Apparatus, for concentrating the heat in any particular place.

The coil of pipes enclosed with an ornamental bronzed case, partly shown in the engraving, with iron or marble top.

Musgrave & Co. are extensively engaged in erecting Hot Water Apparatus for churches, dwelling-houses, warehouses, conservatories, pine pits, &c. They can refer to some of the most extensive buildings in the kingdom which have been satisfactorily heated by them. They will be glad to furnish estimates on favourable terms upon receipt of a plan of the building, and will guarantee the efficiency of any works erected by them.

PRICE LISTS and ESTIMATES for the above, as well as for MUSGRAVE'S PATENT STABLE FITTINGS, MUSGRAVE'S PATENT COWHOUSE and PIGGERY FITTINGS, &c., &c., will be sent free on application to

MUSGRAVE & CO., (Limited), Ann Street Iron Works, Belfast.

Advertisements.

ESTABLISHED AS "THE FLORIST" IN 1848.

PUBLISHED MONTHLY, PRICE ONE SHILLING.

The Florist and Pomologist:

A PICTORIAL MONTHLY MAGAZINE OF FLOWERS, FRUITS, AND GENERAL HORTICULTURE.

NEW SERIES,
WITH
TWO BEAUTIFULLY COLOURED PLATES OF NEW FLOWERS & FRUITS MONTHLY.

The **FLORIST** and **POMOLOGIST**, while sedulously striving to supply the exact information required by **Villa Gardeners and Garden Amateurs**—a class of Cultivators whose technical knowledge of the mysteries of the gardening art is but limited, though their capacity for its enjoyment is unbounded; and to keep **Professional and Commercial Gardeners** respectively posted up as to the **Novelties** which may interest them, seeks at the same time to instruct all classes on the points of Garden Practice upon which modern experience is daily throwing fresh light. While it is thus an indispensable book for the Library or Study of both the Amateur and the Professional Gardener, it may also, on account of its style, its information, and its Illustrations, claim to be admissible to the Drawing-Room or the Boudoir, as a pleasant book of reference on those branches of Horticulture which most interest Lady Gardeners.

The **FLORIST** and **POMOLOGIST** claims to be the leading Illustrated Monthly Magazine of Gardening. The greatest care is taken in the selection and manipulation of subjects for the **Coloured Plates**, the drawings for which are made by the leading Floral and Botanical Artists. The aim and scope of the **Letterpress** is such as to furnish a digest of **Current Information** on all Gardening Matters of interest; to discuss, by the light of experience and the aid of modern science, the **Garden Practice** of the present day; and to give **Seasonable Hints** to those who may need instruction in the management of their gardens, whether devoted to FLOWERS, FRUITS, or VEGETABLES.

The Conductors being aided in their labours by the *élite* of the Gardening profession—a support which they gratefully acknowledge—are enabled to refer with confidence to the sound practical character of the information published in the **FLORIST** and **POMOLOGIST**, emanating as it does from some of the most distinguished Practical and Scientific Horticulturists of the present day, and treating on the most novel and interesting of Horticultural, Floricultural, or Pomological topics.

The **FLORIST** and **POMOLOGIST** is of royal 8vo. size, and is issued on the 1st of every Month. Each number contains 24 pages of Letterpress, and is Illustrated by Two PLATES, beautifully coloured, representing choice **New Flowers** or **New Fruits**, and also by Woodcuts where necessary. It may be ordered through any Bookseller or Newsagent, or if preferred, it may be had through the London Office, from Mr. EDWARD H. MAY, for one year, free by post for Thirteen Shillings.

PUBLISHING OFFICE: 171, FLEET STREET, LONDON, E.C.

Advertisements.

THE GARDENERS' RECORD

AND

JOURNAL OF AGRICULTURE.

The BEST and CHEAPEST PAPER of its kind in Circulation in IRELAND.

SHOULD BE READ BY ALL ENGAGED IN HORTICULTURAL AND AGRICULTURAL PURSUITS.

SUBJECTS :—Gardening and the Science of Horticulture ; Sayings and Doings in London, by a Special Correspondent ; Garden Memoranda, *e.g.*, the Seats of our Resident Landlords and Gentry, with woodcuts ; Calendar of Operations for Kitchen and Flower Gardens, Greenhouse, and Conservatory ; Answers to Correspondents and Household Receipts, &c., &c.

JOURNAL OF AGRICULTURE :—Articles on choice of Seeds ; Chemical Analysis of Manures ; Farm Work ; the Dairy, &c. ; Queries and Answers ; Fairs and Market Notes for week, &c., &c.

YEARLY SUBSCRIPTION (payable in advance), 13s.
Delivered in Town or Country.

SINGLE COPY, 2½d. - - - - **POST FREE, 3d.**

Letters and Manuscripts intended for Publication, and all Advertisements and Money Orders should be addressed to

MR. THOMAS MOORE,
61, MIDDLE ABBEY STREET, DUBLIN.

THE GARDENERS' RECORD & JOURNAL OF AGRICULTURE

IS

PUBLISHED EVERY SATURDAY,

AND MAY BE HAD DIRECT FROM THE OFFICE, OR THROUGH

Messrs. SMITH & SONS, News Agents.

Advertisements.

SHANKS'S PATENT LAWN MOWERS.

UNDER THE PATRONAGE OF
HER MOST GRACIOUS MAJESTY
THE QUEEN

AND MOST OF THE
PRINCIPAL NOBILITY OF
GREAT BRITAIN.

The Improvements introduced into SHANKS'S Lawn Mowers at different times have resulted in these Machines occupying the first place in the market, to which the continued increase in the annual sale bears ample testimony.

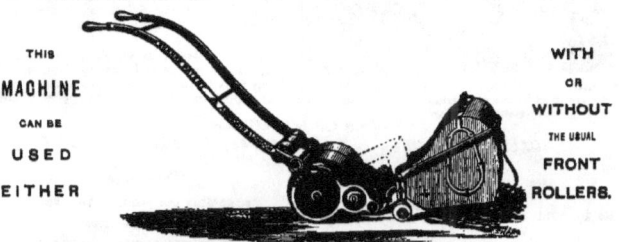

THIS MACHINE CAN BE USED EITHER

WITH OR WITHOUT THE USUAL FRONT ROLLERS.

THE MERITS of these MACHINES are now so well known, and their SUPERIORITY so universally established, that a detailed description is no longer necessary. A. S. & Son would here simply refer to a few of the more prominent features:—The REVOLVING CUTTER is made to be self-sharpening. The SOLE-PLATE or BOTTOM BLADE is made with Two Edges—one in front, as usual, and one in reserve at the back: when the front edge gets worn down, the plate has only to be unscrewed and the unused edge brought to the front. This arrangement enables the cutting parts to last twice as long as in other Machines. A WIND-GUARD is also introduced into their Machine, which prevents the Grass escaping the Box when the Machine is in use during the prevalence of wind.

SHANKS'S PATENT LAWN MOWERS are easy to work, very durable, and silent in working, and have only to be compared with other Lawn Mowers, when the Advantages peculiar to SHANKS'S MACHINES will be at once seen and understood.

PRICES, INCLUDING DELIVERY TO ANY RAILWAY STATION IN THE KINGDOM.

Shanks's Patent Hand Machine, with Silent Movement.

	Easily Worked			Easily Worked
10-inch Machine ... £3 10 0		16-inch Machine ... £6 17 0	By a Man,	
12-inch Machine ... 4 15 0	By a Boy.	19-inch Machine ... 8 5 0	By a Man & a Boy.	
14-inch Machine ... 5 16 0		22-inch Machine ... 9 0 0	By Two Men.	
		24-inch Machine ... 9 10 0		

Shanks's New Patent Pony and Donkey Machine.   Shanks's New Patent Horse Machine.

		If with Patent Delivering Apparatus.			If with Patent Delivering Apparatus
25-inch Machine ... £13 10 0	25s extra.		30-inch Machine ... £20 10 0	30s extra.	
28-inch Machine ... 15 15 0	30s "		36-inch Machine ... 24 0 0	40s "	
30-inch Machine ... 17 0 0	30s "		42-inch Machine ... 28 0 0	40s "	
Silent Movement, 12s 6d extra.			48-inch Machine ... 32 0 0	40s "	
Boots for Pony, 24s per set; ditto for Donkey, 20s per set.			Silent Movement, 20s extra, Boots for Horses, 29s per set.		

SHANKS'S PATENT LAWN MOWERS

Are warranted to give ample satisfaction, and, if not approved of, can be at once returned.

ALEXANDER SHANKS & SON,
DENS IRONWORKS, ARBROATH, & 27, LEADENHALL STREET, LONDON, E.C.

Small Lawn Mowers, Six inch, 30s., Seven inch, 40s., Eight inch, 50s.

Advertisements.

BARNARD, BISHOP, & BARNARDS,
NORFOLK IRON WORKS, NORWICH.

GALVANIZED WROUGHT-IRON FITTINGS,
FOR WIRING WALLS.
FOR THE PURPOSE OF TRAINING FRUIT TREES

On the French system, and as recommended by Mr W. Robinson, F.L.S., in his new work, "The Parks, Promenades, and Gardens of Paris."

By this system nails and shreds are entirely dispensed with, the walls are not injured, and no harbour is afforded to small insects. The tying of the fruit trees is effected in one-fifth of the time required by the old system. The arrangement is so simple that it can easily be applied to any walls by inexperienced hands.

PRICES OF MATERIALS.

GALVANIZED WIRE,

No. 13. 3s per 100 yards.

No. 14. (This is the size most in use for walls.) 2s 6d per 100 yards.

GALVANIZED WROUGHT-IRON EYES.

For guiding the Wires on the Wall.
No. 905. 6d. per dozen.

GALVANIZED RAIDISSEURS,
For Tightening the Wires.
One of these required for each line of Wire.

No. 900. 4s per doz. Wrought-Iron Key for do., 4d.

GALVANISED TERMINATING HOLD-FASTS.
Two of these required for each line of Wire.

No. 908. 2s per doz.

GALVANIZED WROUGHT-IRON ESPALIER TRAINERS,

On the French system, and as recommended by Mr. W. Robinson F.L.S., in his new work, "The Parks, Promenades, and Gardens of Paris."

The arrangement of these Trainers is much improved, and is now rendered so simple that they can be readily fixed by inexperienced hands. The bases of the terminating and intermediate Standards are of Iron, and require neither wood nor stone to attach them to. The wires are usually placed about eight inches apart, but the holes in the Standards can be punched at any required distance.

PRICES OF MATERIALS.

Two required for each length.   Painted.   Galv.
T Iron Terminating Post, with Iron Base and Stay, 4 ft. high, each 12s 6d......17s 0d
  "   "   "   "   "   5 ft. high, "   14s 0d......19s 0d
  "   "   "   "   "   6 ft. high, "   15s 0d......20s 0d
  "   "   "   "   "   7 ft. high, "   19s 0d......26s 0d
  "   "   "   "   "   8 ft. high, "   20s 0d......27s 0d

Usually fixed about 10 ft. apart   Painted.   Galv.
Intermediate Standards, with Anchor feet .... 4 ft. high, each 1s 9d......2s 6d
  "   "   "   "   .... 5 ft. high, "   2s 0d......3s 3d
  "   "   "   "   .... 6 ft. high, "   2s 3d......3s 9d
  "   "   "   "   .... 7 ft. high, "   2s 6d......4s 0d
  "   "   "   "   .... 8 ft. high, "   3s 0d......4s 6d

Galvanised Raidisseurs and Wire, as above, delivered at all the principal Railway Stations, when the amount of Order exceeds £1.

CAN BE OBTAINED OF ANY IRONMONGER.

ILLUSTRATED LISTS OF WIRE NETTING, LAWN MOWERS, AND GARDEN FURNITURE FORWARDED ON APPLICATION.

Advertisements.

UNDER ROYAL  PATRONAGE.

THE ROYAL POTTERY, WESTON-SUPER-MARE.

JOHN MATTHEWS,

MANUFACTURER of TERRA COTTA VASES, FOUNTAINS, ITALIAN BASKETS, RUSTIC FLORAL ARBORETTES. STATUARY, GARDEN POTS (from 2 to 39 inches in diameter, of Superior Quality), withstand Frost, and do not become Green.

PRICE LIST FREE. BOOK OF DRAWINGS, 7d EACH.

ESTABLISHED 35 YEARS.

JAMES BOYD & SONS,
HORTICULTURAL BUILDERS & HEATING ENGINEERS,
PAISLEY, N.B.

CONSERVATORIES, GREENHOUSES, VINERIES, FORCING HOUSES, PITS, and every description of Horticultural Building, Manufactured in Wood or Iron, by Steam-power Machinery, and Erected in any part of the United Kingdom. Manufacturers of Hot Water Apparatus for Heating Churches, Mansions, Warehouses, &c.

PLANS AND ESTIMATES ON APPLICATION.
References can be given to work done in most parts of England, Scotland, and Ireland.
Garden Walls Wired on the most approved principles. Espaliers, Slate Shelves and Cisterns, Garden Seats, Vases, Edgings, &c., and Horticultural Appliances of every description.

F. STEVENSON'S
ABYSSINIAN MIXTURE,

WARRANTED TO DESTROY MEALY BUG, AND ALL INSECTS INFESTING PLANTS.

Unequalled as a Winter Dressing for Vines and Fruit Trees.
Sold by all Nurserymen and Seed Merchants, in Bottles, 1s 6d, 3s, 4s 6d, & 5s 6d each.

INVENTOR AND SOLE MANUFACTURER,
F. STEVENSON, Stamford Street, Altringham, Cheshire.
(Late of Lark Hill, Timperley.)

CHOICEST NEW SEEDS.
ALL THE BEST KINDS IN CULTIVATION.
EVERY GARDEN REQUISITE AND FURNISHING KEPT IN STOCK.
PRIZE FARM SEEDS.
R. B. MATTHEWS,
The Golden Plough Seed Establishment, 65 & 67, Victoria Street,
BELFAST.

NURSERIES, RICHMOND,
ANTRIM ROAD.

☞ Price Catalogues Free on application.

Advertisements.

PERUVIAN GOVERNMENT GUANO.

RICHARDSON BROTHERS & CO.,
OF BELFAST, DUBLIN, AND CORK,
SOLE AGENTS IN IRELAND FOR THE ABOVE GUANO,
(Representing J. Henry, Schroder, & Co., of London,)

INFORM the Public that the Depôts are now being Stocked for the coming Season with ample supplies, and they are prepared to execute orders on the following terms:—

Price £12 10s for lots of not less than 30 Tons; or £13 15s for any smaller quantity, per Ton, in bags, gross weight, ex scale.

Payment—Cash or Bank Draft on Belfast or London. Further Particulars on application.

DISSOLVED PERUVIAN GUANO,
PREPARED BY
OHLENDORFF & CO.,
LONDON, ANTWERP, HAMBURG, AND EMMERICH ON RHINE.
GUARANTEED TO CONTAIN—
Nitrogen equal to 10 per cent. of non-Volatile Ammonia.
20 ,, ,, Soluble } Guano
4 ,, ,, Insoluble } Phosphate.

Price, £14 per Ton for 30 Tons and upwards; £15 per Ton for under 30 Tons.
Delivered free at any of the Depôts in Ireland. Terms—CASH.

This Manure is prepared from *Genuine Peruvian Government Guano*. The result of its special treatment is, that the Ammonia is *fixed*, the Phosphates in the Raw Guano rendered *soluble*, and the Manure brought into the condition of a free, dry powder.

It loses nothing from exposure to the atmosphere, or to the heat of the sun. It is offered to the Farmer with a *Guarantee* of its composition, and is, in fact, the richest, and considering the quality, the cheapest *Guaranteed* Manure at present in the Market. Its fertilising properties are such as will enable the consumer to derive the greatest economical advantage from the use of Guano.

Reference may be made to:—
Dr. HODGES, Chemist to the Chemico-Agricultural Society of Ulster, Belfast;
Dr. CAMERON, Chemist to the Royal Agricultural Society of Ireland, Dublin;
Dr. APJOHN, Professor of Chemistry, T.C., Dublin.

UNDER THE SOLE CONTROL IN IRELAND OF
RICHARDSON BROTHERS & CO.,
BELFAST, DUBLIN, AND CORK.

RICHARDSON BROTHERS & CO.,
AGRICULTURAL CHEMISTS AND LINSEED CRUSHERS,
BELFAST, DUBLIN, AND CORK.

RICHARDSON'S BONE COMPOUND.
RICHARDSON'S SUPERPHOSPHATE.

SPECIAL MANURES.
POTATO MANURE. | **GRASS MANURE.**
FLAX MANURE. | **GRAIN MANURE**
TURNIP MANURE.

RICHARDSON'S LINSEED CAKE AND MEAL.
RICHARDSON'S FEEDING CAKE.

ANALYSES AND PRICES ON APPLICATION.

Advertisements.

FRANCIS RITCHIE & SONS,
MANURE AND FELT MANUFACTURERS,
BELFAST.

PRICE LIST OF MANURES.
Each Bag marked "RITCHIE & SONS."

Per Ton, in Bags.		Per Ton. in Bags.	
Potatoe Manure,	£7 15 0	Crushed Bones,	£9 0 0
Vitriolized Bone Compound,	7 15 0	Bone Meal,	9 2 6
Grass Manure,	7 15 0	Bone Flour,	9 5 0
Grain Manure,	7 15 0	Nitrate of Soda,	Variable.
Sulphate of Ammonia,	Variable.		

Our Agents can supply any quantity at above prices, with the addition of the lowest possible carriage.

BELFAST CHEMICAL MANURE WORKS.

June, 1874.

SIR,—In again soliciting your orders, we do so with the conviction that we are in a position to offer you a genuine good Manure that must produce satisfactory results. We feel that we are warranted in saying so much from the fact of our being the largest and oldest Manure Manufacturers in this country, and also from the fact of our being in a position to procure raw material abundantly and cheaply. Our long-continued experience and knowledge of the chemical composition and value of various materials enable us to select and combine in the most efficient manner, thus producing good and valuable fertilizers. We profess to manufacture cheap but not low-priced Manures, and, from the extent of our production, are enabled to sell at a moderate profit per ton, thus giving to Agriculturists, Manures second to none in the kingdom, quality and price considered.

The length of time our Manures have now been before the public, and the rapidly increasing demand, are the best guarantees we can give of their value, and of the estimation in which they are held.

We can with confidence recommend our

VITRIOLIZED BONE COMPOUND,

which produces not only a heavy and healthy crop, but adds considerably to the fertility of the soil for the ensuing crops. The best results may be expected when used in the proportion of 4 to 5 cwt. per statute acre, with half the usual quantity of Farm-yard Manure; should Farm-yard Manure not be available, double the above quantity of Bone Compound should be used, when, if the soil naturally contain sufficient vegetable matter, equally good crops are likely to be obtained.

The Vitriolised Bone Compound should be intimately mixed with from four to five times its bulk of dry ashes or earth, and applied over the Farm-yard Manure, the whole covered lightly with earth, so as to prevent contact of the seed with the Manure.

POTATO MANURE.

We have manufactured a POTATO MANURE, made in accordance with the composition of the Potato Plant, which we now offer, with the conviction that, if applied properly, either alone or with half Farm-yard Manure, it must produce an early and good crop of Potatoes, in many instances protecting them to a considerable extent from disease. From experiments conducted both in the laboratory and in the field, we feel we are warranted in thus speaking so confidently of this Manure, which only needs to be tried in order to prove our statements. We recommend either 10 cwt. of the Potatoe Manure to be applied to the statute acre when used alone, or 5 cwt. and half Farm-yard Manure, applied in the ordinary way.

GRASS MANURE

Applied early in spring, at the rate of from 3 to 4 cwt. per statute acre, as a top-dressing for grass, &c., greatly increases and improves the produce, and enables the cutting to be made two or three weeks earlier than usual. Applied as a top-dressing, it should be sown broadcast, immediately before, during, or after rain.

GRAIN MANURE

improves the straw, and gives a greater yield of grain; and the extra straw will repay the cost of the Manure. Apply at the rate of five cwt. to the acre.

For the purpose of supplying a pure article of

BONES,

we have erected new and powerful Patent machinery, by which we can grind Bones TO ANY REQUIRED DEGREE OF FINENESS. The finer the grind the quicker the action of Bones, and we would call attention to our

BONE FLOUR,

as a most efficient and permanent Manure. Orders at all times shall have our best attention, and we solicit a trial, knowing that the results shall be such as must secure increasing orders or the future.

FRANCIS RITCHIE & SONS.

Advertisements.

THE JOURNAL OF HORTICULTURE,
EDITED BY
G. W. JOHNSON, F.R.H.S., and ROBERT HOGG, LL.D., F.L.S.

Is Published Weekly, Price 3d,

AND IS

AMPLY ILLUSTRATED WITH EXCELLENT WOOD ENGRAVINGS.
36 PAGES.

AFTER a prosperous career extending over a quarter of a century, the JOURNAL OF HORTICULTURE still continues to take the lead as a Family Paper in Rural Homes, on all subjects connected with THE GARDEN and THE HOMESTEAD, including the Poultry-Yard, the Dovecote, the Aviary, and the Apiary.

The JOURNAL OF HORTICULTURE has the largest circulation of any Gardening Periodical in existence.

A New Volume commences in the first week of January, and the first week of July, annually.

TERMS OF SUBSCRIPTION.

The JOURNAL may be had of all Booksellers, and at the Railway Book Stalls, Price 3d; and, if sent direct from the Office, free by Post, on prepayment of the following terms:—Three Months, 3s 9d; Six Months, 7s 6d; Twelve Months, 15s.

A Specimen number will be sent from the Office, Post-free, on receipt of 3½d in Stamps.

OFFICE—171, FLEET STREET, LONDON, E.C.
E. H. MAY, Publisher.

USED IN THE ROYAL GARDENS,
And Principal Nurseries and Gardens throughout the United Kingdom, with the most successful results.

FOWLER'S HORTICULTURAL REQUISITES.

GARDENERS' INSECTICIDE destroys and prevents, without the slightest stain or injury to the most delicate Plant or Root, every Insect, Blight, and Mildew to which Plants and Trees are subject. It is easily applied, by dipping, syringing, sponging, or as a winter dressing; does not require cleansing off with water; and gives the foliage a bright, clean, and healthy appearance. *Price 1s 6d, 3s, 5s 6d, and 10s per Jar.*

TOBACCO POWDER, for dusting Plants and Trees infested with Insects, Blights, and Mildews. It is intended for those who prefer the application of a powder, and will be found a more effectual remedy than the ordinary "Duty Free Ground Tobacco." *Price 1s, 2s 6d, 5s, and 10s per Tin.*

STANDEN'S MANURE, or GARDENERS' AND AMATEURS' FRIEND, is specially prepared for the use of exhibitors and others who aim to excel in the culture of Flowers, Fruit, and Vegetables. It promotes a rapid, healthy, and finely-developed growth, with the highest excellence of colour, size and quality. *Price 1s, 2s 6d, 5s 6d, 10s 6d, and 21s per Tin.*

GARDEN MANURE.—This Manure is specially prepared to meet the demand for a thoroughly efficient and reliable Manure for garden purposes, at a moderate price. The effectiveness and permanence of its action is much greater than Guano or Farmyard Manure, and renders its use in the garden a matter of economy.—*Price, in Bags, 112 lbs., 24s; 56 lbs., 13s; in Cases, 28 lbs., 7s; 14 lbs., 3s 9d; 7 lbs., 2s; 3 lbs., 1s each.*

MEALY BUG DESTROYER.—A special preparation for the safe, easy, and complete eradication of this most troublesome of Stove House Plant pests. It is instant destruction to both insects and ova, easily and cleanly applied, and will not stain or injure the foliage. *Price 1s, 2s 6d, 5s, and 10s per Bottle.*

Testimonials from the most Eminent Authorities.
SOLD BY NURSERYMEN, SEEDSMEN, AND CHEMISTS.

SOLE MANUFACTURERS:
G. & T. FOWLER, 35, GREAT DOVER STREET, LONDON.

www.ingramcontent.com/pod-product-compliance
Lightning Source LLC
Chambersburg PA
CBHW020927230426
43666CB00008B/1593